WHAT YOUR PASTOR WON'T TELL YOU

BUT I CAN BECAUSE I'M RETIRED

MARSHALL DAVIS

ISBN: 9781720258674 (paperback)

Imprint: Independently published

CONTENTS

INTRODUCTION

WHY YOUR PASTOR WON'T TELL YOU

There is a secret your pastor is not telling you. In fact he has a lot of secrets. A large part of a pastor's job is to keep confidences - things that pastors cannot even tell their own spouse. People have privately told me things that they have not told their own families. I have secrets that I will take to my grave. That is probably why people have been willing to confide in me over the years. Time has proven that I - like most pastors - will not reveal anything spoken in confidence.

So this book is not a "tell all" book, like ghost-written memoirs by celebrities and politicians. Members of churches I have served have no need to worry. I am not going to be spilling any personal secrets shared in counseling sessions. There is no need for me to change the names in this book to protect the guilty ... I mean the innocent. This is not my *Peyton Place*, which was a book based on the lives of real people in Gilmanton, New Hampshire. The people in my small town of Sandwich, New Hampshire, or the other towns I have served, need not fear. This is not that type of book.

But I will be sharing personal things about what it is like being a pastor. This is the theme of the first section, "What Your Pastor Won't Tell You about the Ministry." I will explore how ministers deal with stress, financial difficulties, criticism, church politics and misunderstanding. I will describe the toll that ministry takes on ministers and their families. I will be addressing issues of pastor burnout, clergy misconduct, denominational misbehavior, as well as the difficulty of being the head of a religious organization composed entirely of volunteers. It is like pushing water uphill with a rake!

I will also deal with serious issues like sexual misconduct – including sexual assault - and the struggle of LGBTQ people. I will be honest about such things – without betraying confidences. This book addresses the emotional aspects of being a pastor – things that a pastor normally would not share, except with a therapist or perhaps a Pastoral Relations Committee, but often not even there. (Such committees are not always as confidential as pastors might hope.)

I will not only be sharing the difficult aspects of ministry but also the good parts. Pastors tend not to tell their people about the blessings of being a pastor. Although the financial rewards of ministry are not great, the pay is usually sufficient for those pastors able to find fulltime employment. I am retired comfortably now due to the excellent retirement benefits provided by my denomination.

My family has always had good healthcare. Even before we had medical insurance, the Baptists were taking care of my family. The Baptist Hospital East of Louisville, Kentucky, did not bill me one cent for hospital care involving the birth of our first two children. That included a hospital stay for a blood clot that my wife suffered during her first pregnancy and our second son's hospital stay due to exposure to tuberculosis. The care was free because I was a student at the local Baptist seminary. How many other professions can testify to treatment like that?

Furthermore I have been blessed to share the most meaningful moments of peoples' lives for over forty years. At the same time I have been able to devote time to exploring my own spiritual life. As difficult as pastoral ministry can be at times, it is still a wonderful vocation. I am very grateful, and I – like most pastors – do not express my gratitude enough.

Even though I will start off this book talking about church life, much of this book is not about church. I will talk about theological and spiritual matters, including the Bible, Christian doctrine, Church history, and Christian ethics. I will expose things that most church members do not know about the content of their religion.

In other words, your pastor is not telling everything. At least not in the sense of the courtroom oath, "the truth, the whole truth, and nothing but the truth." She is not lying to you. She is just not telling you everything she knows. This book is my attempt to tell you what your pastor won't.

Your pastor learned a lot of things in seminary or divinity school that she can't bring herself to talk about from the pulpit. She might touch upon some of these uncomfortable truths in private conversations or in small Bible Study groups, where a level of trust has been established. But you will never hear them elaborated in sermons.

Why? There are a lot of reasons for it. From my personal experience and talking to other pastors, I have identified four main reasons pastors will not tell the whole truth: Fear, Privacy, Ignorance, and a Change of Heart. Often these reasons overlap.

FEAR

First is **fear**. Your pastor may be hesitant to tell the truth for fear of losing his job. Speaking the truth might jeopardize his livelihood. This is a very big concern, especially when the financial support of a family is concerned.

In the 1992 film *A Few Good Men*, there is a courtroom scene where an attorney, Lieutenant Junior Grade Daniel Kaffee (played by Tom Cruise), confronts Marine Colonel Nathan Jessup (played by Jack Nicholson) who is on the witness stand. At issue is whether the colonel ordered a Code Red, a violent extrajudicial punishment which resulted in the death of a fellow Marine. Here is the exchange:

LTJG Kaffee: Colonel Jessup! Did you order the Code Red?

Judge Randolph: You don't have to answer that question!

Col Jessup: I'll answer the question. You want answers?

LTJG Kaffee: I think I'm entitled to them.

Col Jessup: You want answers?!

LTJG Kaffee: I want the truth!

Col Jessup: YOU CAN'T HANDLE THE TRUTH!

Your pastor likely withholds information because he thinks that you cannot handle the truth. But he won't admit that unless he is under oath. Pastors withhold many things that they have learned in their studies because they believe it is best for the church - and for them - if some things are left unspoken. If he told you the truth, chances are you would vote with your feet… and leave.

Your pastor's fears are not unfounded. New research has revealed that the chief reason people leave a church is because of a change in the church's teachings. A 2018 survey by LifeWay Research has found that more people are apt to leave a church if the church's beliefs change than all other reasons combined.

Among those open to changing churches, only 5% said they would leave their church because of a change in music style. 9% would leave over a difference in political views. 12% would leave if the pastor left. 48% said they would change churches if they moved. But a whopping 53% named a change of doctrine as the reason they would leave a church.[1]

As Scott McConnell, executive director of LifeWay Research, interpreted the data, "Mess with the music and people may grumble. Mess with the theology and they're out the door."[2] That is strong incentive for not upsetting the theological apple cart.

Churches are struggling with the decline of church membership as older generations die off and the "Nones" (those who check the box "None of the Above" in surveys about religious affiliation) increase. Repeated surveys confirm what pastors already know. Every succeeding generation – from the Baby Boomers (born 1946 to 1964), to Gen X (born 1965 to 1983) to Millennials (born 1984 to 1998) and now Gen Z (those born 1999 to 2015) - is less likely than the previous generation to darken the doors of our churches.

Gen Z is the least religious generation to date. A 2017 Barna study reveals that 34 percent of Gen Z identify their religious affiliation as either atheist, agnostic or none. Teens 13-18 years old are twice as likely as adults to say they are atheist. Just three in five 13 to 18 year-olds say they are some kind of Christian (59 percent).[3]

A pastor does not want anything to decease the ranks of those still attending church. Therefore he will keep silent about some things in order to stem the tide of decline and maintain the status quo.

Most Christians' faith is based upon an understanding of the Bible and Christian doctrine that they learned in Sunday School. Their basic theology has not changed much since childhood. It is not because they were not willing to learn if given the opportunity. Pastors have generally not taught the complex and difficult truths about Christianity. They have found it easier not to raise the hard theological and biblical issues.

Even though Jesus said that we have to become like little children to enter the Kingdom of God, we are not supposed to remain children in our understanding and knowledge. We are supposed to grow in wisdom, as Jesus did. (Luke 2:52) We are exhorted to grow in our salvation. (I Peter 2:2)

Paul rebukes the members of church in Corinth for not growing in their faith, "But I, brothers, could not address you as spiritual people, but as people of the flesh, as infants in Christ. I fed you with milk, not solid food, for you were not ready for it. And even now you are not yet ready...." (I Corinthians 2:1-2)

The prolonged adolescence of the average Christian is the reason for the distrust of education among conservative Christians. Learning can be dangerous to your faith. It is a worry of many devout parents that their children will lose their religion when they go away to college, or even sooner.

That is the impetus behind the Christian home schooling movement. If devout parents can keep their little ones away from dangerous ideas like evolution and birth control, then they might be able to keep them in the fold. But parents cannot keep them away from knowledge forever. When they finally come in contact with new ideas, then it shakes their childhood faith – and rightly so.

I found this to be true even of seminary students. I was blessed to be raised in a mainline church. I attended a private boarding school and an excellent liberal arts college. During my education I was exposed to many challenging ideas from an early age. But many of my fellow students in seminary were not so fortunate.

Most of my fellow seminarians came from conservative churches and conservative homes. They had never heard anything but a literalistic interpretation of the Bible and a legalistic understanding of Christian doctrine and ethics. When they were exposed to modern biblical scholarship and theology, they were thrown off balance. It produced a crisis of faith for many of them.

That experience is true to a lesser extent even for seminarians from more liberal backgrounds. Some things are just not talked about in mainline churches or Christian homes. There are consequences to following the old maxim that politics or religion are not to be discussed in "polite company." (At least opposing opinions in politics and religion are not to be entertained.) Churches are polite company. At least they pretend to be. Church leaders tend to keep their churches homogeneous by not presenting dissenting opinions, except to discredit them. Introducing controversial ideas could upset the delicate balance of church and family life.

Speaking truths, which call into question the cherished Sunday School beliefs of faithful church members, can cause problems for pastors. It might diminish the number of bottoms on the pews and dollars in the plates. "Discretion is the better part of valor," as Falstaff said. Discretion, more often than not, translates into silence.

Fear is a factor in the decision of some pastors not to share what they have learned in seminary and in their ongoing scholarly pursuits. They may be afraid of conservative backlash from those who view unconventional interpretations of Scripture or doctrine as a threat to the purity of the gospel. That is especially true in conservative churches.

Even progressive churches often have a sizable contingent of people who hold to a traditional understanding of Christianity. The church is by nature a conservative institution that does not deal with change well. Christians – especially conservative Christians – are wary of new ideas. New ideas cannot – by definition - be the Old Time Religion or the Faith of our Fathers. Unusual ideas carry the scent of heresy.

Questioning key doctrines brings with it the fear of losing one's salvation, along with the threat of hell and damnation. This is weighty stuff for a new pastor to face right out of seminary. For that reason many pastors keep silent. Pastors who introduce innovative understandings of Christianity can be labeled liberals, which to traditional Christians mean that one has departed from "the gospel once for all delivered to the saints" (Jude 3). In evangelical Christianity if one does not hold to certain "fundamentals" of the faith, including a literal interpretation of scripture, then one is not really a Christian.

PRIVACY

A second reason pastors are reluctant to tell the whole truth is **privacy**. This is especially true concerning the first chapter of this book: "What Your Pastor Won't Tell You About the Ministry." There are a lot of things that pastors do not feel comfortable sharing with people in their congregations.

Pastors tend to be private people. As we will see, they tend not to have close friends. They are required to be friendly with the whole congregation. Indeed they have a very large number of "church friends." Nobody knows as many people in the church as the pastor does! But when it comes to people that pastors are willing to share their innermost thoughts and feelings with, they have very few, if any.

One thing that pastors keep private is their feeling of incompetency in ministry. As we will see in Chapter 1, most pastors – as much as 90% according to one survey - feel they were not adequately trained to cope with the demands of ministry. In the pulpit they might come across as experts in biblical, theological, and ethical matters. They sprinkle their sermons with Greek and Hebrew words and quote famous theologians. But the truth is that they do not know as much as you think.

Many feel insecure about their ability to teach others what they have learned in seminary and in their ongoing studies, especially if these insights raise questions about traditional Christianity. The reality is that pastors are not experts in biblical criticism, theology or church history. Pastors are generalists. We are trained to be general practitioners. We have learned a lot of information about a wide range of subjects, but most of us are not specialists in any one area.

That makes the presentation of complex biblical scholarship and theological subtleties very difficult for most pastors. Few pastors feel qualified – nor do they have the time – to delve into the depths of higher criticism or theological profundities. They barely have time to research and write a good sermon! Therefore many pastors deem it wiser to avoid the whole enterprise.

Not only do pastors not feel academically equipped, they do not feel inspired to fight fundamentalists in their congregations. The price is usually too high. So they choose to keep silent. For that reason the truths that every seminary student knows never make it to people sitting in the pews on Sunday morning. It is safer for pastors to concentrate on other things.

In short, if your pastor is silent about certain matters it is because there are dynamics in churches and denominations that make it easier to take this route. If he is silent he is more likely to keep his job ... along with his healthcare, his housing, and his pension. That is a big incentive. But I am retired, so I have nothing to lose. I can tell you the truth.

Don't take me for a coward who only speaks when it is safe to do so. I have taken the high road during my ministry and have the battle scars to prove it. I know the cost, and for that reason I do not look down on those who choose to tread the safer path. I spoke up for truth (as I saw it) a decade ago and it cost me my job, my denominational affiliation, and many friendships. The stress caused me to leave ministry for a year.

My mental health suffered. A therapist diagnosed me with PTSD – caused not by military combat but by church conflict. I have paid my dues. I spoke like a prophet when I had everything to lose, and I received the prophet's reward (Matthew 5:11-12). I am blessed now to have the freedom to speak so that my fellow pastors don't have to. I can say things that my colleagues in fulltime ministry wish they could say, but can't. I don't blame them. I was one of them.

Nothing I will say in this book is radical or outside the scope of mainstream biblical scholarship or Christian theology. In fact my views are representative of mainline Protestantism. Everything I say in this book has been well-known to seminary trained clergy for over a hundred years. It is well-established scholarly consensus found in countless commentaries and theology books written by scholars from the best theological schools in this country and the world.

This approach was taught in every class I have attended over the last fifty years - in college, seminary and in continuing education. These would include American Baptist institutions such as Northern Baptist Theological Seminary, Eastern Baptist

Theological Seminary (now Palmer Theological Seminary), Andover Newton Theological School, Pittsburgh Theological Seminary, and Regent's Park College, which is part of Oxford University. Not long ago it was also the consensus opinion of professors teaching at my alma mater, the Southern Baptist Theological Seminary, where I earned my graduate degrees. Sadly that is no longer the case.

In the interest of full disclosure I will explain my religious background. I am an ordained American Baptist minister who has served churches affiliated with the American Baptist, Southern Baptist, and United Methodist denominations. I received my undergraduate degree in Religion from Denison University, a liberal arts college, when it was still affiliated (although tenuously) with the American Baptist Convention (previously known as the Northern Baptist Convention and now called the American Baptist Churches USA).

From there I went on to earn Master of Divinity and Doctor of Ministry degrees from the Southern Baptist Theological Seminary in Louisville, Kentucky. Everything I will write in this book was common knowledge at the Baptist institutions of higher learning that I attended. At that time Baptist theological education was both broad and deep, drawing upon the best of biblical and theological scholarship in America and Europe through the centuries and across denominations.

But there has been a big shift in theological education in the last thirty years. One reason why some pastors will not tell you the things I say in this book is because they were never taught them. There was a radical change in theological education in the 1980's. Just as there has been a bifurcation and radicalization in American politics into liberal and conservative wings, so has the same thing happened in American theological education. Today the largest theological seminaries are conservative and hold to fundamentalist beliefs as a matter of conviction rather than scholarly research. Consequently the things every seminary graduate used to know are no longer widely known.

This is represented by the dramatic change that has occurred in the Southern Baptist Convention. This shift is called either the Conservative Resurgence or the Fundamentalist Takeover of the denomination, depending on whether you were on the winning or losing side of the struggle. As a result of the shift in denominational power in favor of biblical inerrancy, those who taught higher biblical criticism and theological moderation (called liberalism by its opponents) were purged from faculties and replaced with professors willing to sign their names to strict doctrinal creeds. As a result of this curtailment of academic freedom, students graduating from these schools during the last thirty years became less knowledgeable.

IGNORANCE

This is the third reason why your pastor is not telling you the truth: **ignorance**. They aren't preaching it because they weren't taught it. Evangelicals are not as knowledgeable as they used to be. During the last few decades the term "evangelical" has been redefined.

When I was in seminary we used to joke that an evangelical was a fundamentalist who had been to college. What we meant is that evangelicals learned not to take the Bible literally. Now the fundamentalists *own* the Christian colleges and seminaries and have turned them into bastions of Fundamentalism, which they have renamed Evangelicalism. For those in the mainstream media Evangelical = Fundamentalist + conservative Republican. It wasn't always that way.

The word "evangelical" used to refer to a personal pietistic faith in Christ and an evangelistic attitude (think Jimmy Carter). The word could represent people from a wide range of theological perspectives. Now the term has become synonymous with theological fundamentalism (think Jerry

Falwell). What used to be called Fundamentalism in the early twentieth century is called Evangelicalism in the early twenty-first century.

This conservative shift in theological education in the Southern Baptist Convention did not affect the mainline Protestant denominations and seminaries, which continued to adhere to the highest standards of biblical and theological scholarship. But it did affect the rapidly growing number of independent and nondenominational churches and megachurches, whose pastors are trained at evangelical schools.

The fundamentalist Liberty University today boasts of being the largest Christian college in the country. The ten largest seminaries in the country are all evangelical Protestant. Half of them are Southern Baptist-affiliated. The proliferation of unaccredited online schools has added to this situation, as academic standards became more difficult for a church's Pastor Search Committee to ascertain. Fundamentalism has become the new face of American Christianity, due in no small part to the influence of Evangelicalism in Christian radio and television.

Within mainline (and increasingly sidelined) Protestant denominations, the decline of church membership has made it difficult for small churches (which are 90% of all churches) to call seminary trained clergy. Church membership has declined rapidly, and so have church budgets and ministers' salaries. As a result pastors' salaries are insufficient to meet basic living expenses and pay off student loans accumulated from traditional seminary education. Therefore fewer fully trained pastors are entering the ministry.

In order to fill the pulpits of shrinking churches, declining denominations have relaxed educational standards for their clergy. It used to be required for all mainline clergy to have a four year undergraduate degree followed by a three-year Master of Divinity degree. Now many clergy have only an undergraduate degree, which is not necessarily in Religion, Bible or Theology. Increasing numbers of pastors do not even have that much education.

There was a time when the pastor of the village church was one of the most educated people in town. Now it is not unusual to find clergy with only a high school education, supplemented with a few in-house theological courses approved by their denomination.

Don't get me wrong. These pastors are mostly fine, sincere, intelligent, self-educated, dedicated leaders who are doing a wonderful job under difficult circumstances. I count many of them as my friends and colleagues. My observation is that they often do a better job than their seminary trained counterparts. Today's church would be far poorer without them.

But their lack of education may be the reason they are not telling you the truth. They might not know the truth. To put it bluntly (which I will do a lot in this book), uneducated or undereducated pastors don't know what they don't know. When one has not been given all the information, it is much more difficult to preach "the truth, the whole truth, and nothing but the truth."

This lack of knowledge is not the fault of these pastors. It is the fault of a compromised denominational and educational system. I hope this book will goad all pastors into further education, and goad their churches into demanding it. I also hope it will cause more pastors to break their silence.

CHANGE OF HEART

The fourth reason that pastors do not tell the truth is that some have had a **change of heart**. They have changed their minds about what is true. They have rejected what they had previously learned in college, seminary, and personal study. They have retreated into a pre-critical understanding of scripture, theology, and ethics. Some have purposely chosen not to pursue seminary education so as not to be challenged by uncomfortable ideas.

A good example of this is the decision of Billy Graham to embrace the infallibility of the Bible in matters of science and history in spite of evidence to the contrary. This story is told vividly by Graham's long-time friend, and former fellow evangelist, Charles Templeton in his book *Farewell to God.*

Although already a successful evangelist – as successful at that time as his friend Billy Graham – Templeton had unanswered questions and felt the need for more education. So he decided to enter seminary. Although he had not finished high school, through the intervention of George Pidgeon, moderator of the United Church of Canada, he was admitted to Princeton Theological Seminary as a "special student."

He urged his friend Billy to join him in obtaining a theological education. Billy had only a BA in Anthropology from Wheaton College at the time. (This remained the highest degree Graham ever earned.) Shortly before Templeton was to enroll at Princeton, he met his friend in New York City for a heart-to-heart discussion. They spent the better part of two days closeted in a room in the Taft Hotel. Templeton describes their conversation this way:

> All our differences came to a head in a discussion which, better than anything I know, explains Billy Graham and his phenomenal

success as an evangelist. In the course of our conversation I said, "But, Billy, it's simply not possible any longer to believe, for instance, the biblical account of creation. The world wasn't created over a period of days a few thousand years ago; it has evolved over millions of years. It's not a matter of speculation; it's demonstrable fact."

"I don't accept that," Billy said. "And there are reputable scholars who don't."

"Who are these scholars?" I said. "Men in conservative Christian colleges."

"Most of them, yes," he said. "But that's not the point. I believe the Genesis account of creation because it's in the Bible. I've discovered something in my ministry: when I take the Bible literally, when I proclaim it as the Word of God, my preaching has power. When I stand on the platform and say, 'God says,' or 'the Bible says,' the Holy Spirit uses me. There are results. Wiser men than you and I have been arguing questions like this for centuries. I don't have the time or the intellect to examine all sides of each theological dispute, so I've decided, once and for all, to stop questioning and accept the Bible as God's Word."

"But, Billy," I protested, "you can't do that. You don't dare stop thinking about the most important question in life. Do it and you begin to die. It's intellectual suicide."

"I don't know about anybody else," he said, "but I've decided that that's the path for me." [4]

A few months after this encounter, Billy Graham held his evangelistic campaign in Los Angeles, which catapulted him to international prominence overnight.

Billy Graham has described this decision as the turning point in his life. In his autobiography *Just as I Am*, he records the decision he made shortly after this hotel meeting with Templeton. He was staying at the Forest Home Christian Camp in California before beginning his crusade in Los Angeles. He walked out into the woods, set his Bible on a tree stump, and prayed. Graham writes:

> The exact wording of my prayer is beyond recall, but it must have echoed my thoughts: "O God! There are many things in this book I do not understand. There are many problems with it for which I have no solution. There are many seeming contradictions. There are some areas in it that do not seem to correlate with modern science. I can't answer some of the philosophical

WHAT YOUR PASTOR WON'T TELL YOU

and psychological questions Chuck and others are raising."

I was trying to be on the level with God, but something remained unspoken. At last the Holy Spirit freed me to say it. "Father, I am going to accept this as Thy Word — by *faith*! I'm going to allow faith to go beyond my intellectual questions and doubts, and I will believe this to be Your inspired Word!" [5]

No one would doubt the success of Billy Graham as a preacher and evangelist. And no one would doubt his sincerity and integrity in fulfilling his ministry. But neither should we doubt that at a crucial moment he decided not to pursue greater understanding of the nature of God's Word, but to uncritically embrace a theory of biblical inspiration that he had learned as a teenager at Bob Jones College.

By his own admission he accepted a particular interpretation of Scripture *on faith* without researching it and testing it to see if it was true. By the words he used in his prayer, he seemed unaware that what he was accepting "by faith" that day was not the Bible but a nineteenth century theory *about* the Bible.

Ironically this is a theory not supported by the Bible itself. In effect he chose to unconditionally accept a questionable theory about scripture rather than trust the testimony of scripture itself, based on the best biblical scholarship available. Graham was successful beyond his wildest dreams, but the price he paid, as his friend said, was intellectual suicide.

Many other pastors have made the same type of decision, but without the same dramatic results. They have decided not to pursue a theological education or study the nature and origin of the Bible on their own. Others, who received a theological education, decided to abandon what they had learned in favor of a simpler prescientific worldview.

Why have they done this? The reasons discussed above - fear and insecurity - probably have something to do with it. I have noticed that once a person is out of the academic setting, the conservative culture of the church gradually reclaims a pastor until he decides that what he had learned in seminary was not really true after all.

One tends to take on the beliefs of those we associate with most. After one leaves the insulated atmosphere of academia and takes up residence on the church field, it is easy to revert back to the mindset we had before we were exposed to higher education. We can easily retreat into a church's groupthink, thereby facilitating our acceptance by the congregation. This is often not done intentionally; it happens naturally and incrementally. Nevertheless it is a form of self-deceit.

We convince ourselves that we were mistaken to accept the expertise of our seminary professors. We begin to revisit and rationalize our previous beliefs. We start to think that our professors were out of touch with the average Christian in the pews. We conclude that much learning has driven them mad, as Festus said about the apostle Paul. Their learning has led them into apostasy, and it almost ensnared us! Thank the Lord, we came to our senses and came "back to the Bible" before it was too late!

If our seminary education is not reinforced by a regimen of continuing education and personal scholarly study, it is easy to slip back into the simplistic motto of "God Said It, I Believe It, That Settles It," without examining too closely the presuppositions and logic of that slogan.

For whatever reasons, many pastors suspend their ongoing search for greater light as they adjust to the demanding life of pastoral ministry. In my mind this is not a surrender to the God of Truth or the One who said, "I am the Way, the Truth and the Life." It is a surrender to ignorance.

As great as Billy Graham was, just imagine what Dr. Graham could have accomplished with his oratorical skills and charisma if he had the courage to further his education and receive an earned doctorate rather than an honorary one. He could have ushered Evangelicalism into the twentieth century rather than keep it bound to the nineteenth century.

Pastoral silence on important biblical, theological and ethical issues is no longer acceptable. It is responsible for the dumbing down of Christianity in America. In this age of "fake news" we now have a fake gospel. In this era of "alternative facts," we now have Christians who do not know the facts about their own religion. American Christianity is daily becoming less knowledgeable about its own scriptures, theology, history and ethics.

The purpose of this book is to call attention to things that every pastor used to know, and every Christian ought to know, but which now is seldom taught in churches. I think that Christians should be told the truth. Furthermore I believe they can handle the truth.

1

WHAT YOUR PASTOR WON'T TELL YOU ABOUT THE MINISTRY

Being a pastor is tough work. It is not necessarily tougher than some other professions – such as physicians, firefighters or police officers - but it is tougher than many church members think. Your pastor won't tell you that, so I will.

Ministry is not physically demanding the way that manual labor is. In fact one of the major health problems of clergy is obesity. A 2015 study from Baylor University finds that more than a third of American clergy are obese. But being a pastor is more emotionally and psychologically demanding than most jobs.

There is a misconception about ministry – that it is a relatively easy profession. After all, pastors only work one day a week, right? Going out of worship one Sunday, a mom asked her young daughter if she knew where I lived. Her response was to point to the door at the front of the sanctuary. Every Sunday I came out of that door to lead the worship service, so she assumed that I lived somewhere in the bowels of the church building and emerged only to preach!

There are a lot of adults who think about ministry in the same way. It is understandable since most church members only see their pastor for that one hour. A colleague of mine who, who eventually was forced from his position and left the ministry, was confronted by a member of his church's board of trustees. The trustee growled that he had calculated how much they were paying him *per sermon*, by dividing his total compensation by 52. This church officer assumed that the pastor only worked Sunday morning. The rest of the week was spent researching and writing the Sunday sermon!

The truth is that a pastor typically only gets one day off a week, and sometimes not even that! She is always on call for emergencies, and those "emergencies" seem to happen disproportionately on the pastor's day off. Pastoral ministry is at least a six-day-a-week job. A 2010 LifeWay Research survey found that 65 percent of senior pastors work 50 or more hours a week. 8 percent report working 70 or more hours.[6] The detrimental consequences of such a work schedule on a pastor's mental and emotional health has been known for decades.

In his 2006 book *Clergy Burnout: Recovering from the 70 hour Work Week and Other Self-Defeating Practices,* Fred Lehr mentions an oft-quoted study done by Fuller Theological Seminary. It reported that 90% of pastors work more than 46 hours per week. 80 percent believe that pastoral ministry is affecting their families negatively. 33 percent say that "being in ministry is clearly a hazard to my family." 75 percent reported a significant crisis due to stress at least once in their ministry. 50 percent felt unable to meet the needs of the ministry. 90 percent felt they were not adequately trained to cope with the ministry demands placed upon them. 40 percent reported at least one serious conflict with at least one parishioner at least once a month. 70 percent of pastors do not have someone they would consider a close friend. 70 percent had a lower self-image since beginning pastoral ministry.[7]

A 2014 LifeWay Research survey commissioned by Focus on the Family reports that nearly 1 in 4 pastors (23 percent) acknowledge they have "personally struggled with mental illness," and half of those pastors said the illness had been medically diagnosed.[8] More than half of evangelical and Reformed pastors told the Schaeffer Institute in 2015 and 2016 that they don't have any good and true friends (58 percent). About the same number reported they can't meet their church's unrealistic expectations

(52 percent). Close to a third battle discouragement (34 percent) or depression/fear of inadequacy (35 percent) on a regular basis. [9] The Schaeffer Institute also reports that 80 percent of seminary and Bible school graduates will leave the ministry within five years.[10]

The good news is that these statistics might be exaggerated. In a May 9, 2018 article in *The Christian Century* entitled "The Pastors are Alright," Amy Frykholm makes the case that some of these oft-quoted surveys are faulty in their methodology. Furthermore some are outdated. For example the study done by Fuller Theological Seminary quoted by Lehr above is from the 1980's. She points to more recent and larger studies, such as the Barna Group's 2017 "The State of Pastors" and data from the Clergy Health Initiative at Duke University.

But even the Barna study revealed that 30 percent of clergy are at risk of burnout. The Clergy Health Initiative study found that nine to eleven percent of clergy deal with depression, which is four percent higher than the general population. According to CHI 12 to 15 percent of clergy report feeling very or extremely isolated.[11] These are warning signs of suicide. The recent spate of suicides by high profile pastors and their family members add to the perception that pastors are at risk.

Another recent large-scale study at the Flourishing in Ministry Project at the University of Notre Dame reports that clergy are doing better than previously thought, but some trends are not encouraging. For one thing women and people of color in ministry report having more mental and emotional health problems than white men. Barna's research likewise shows that female pastors are twice as likely (38%) as male pastors (20%) to feel exhausted frequently.

On top of that, ministry is becoming more difficult as society changes. Matt Bloom of the Flourishing in Ministry Project says, "Being a pastor is much more difficult than it used to be. I think that the ecosystem is not as conducive to flourishing: the demands are higher, the support systems are not as strong. As churches have seen their membership rolls drop, they have responded in ways that have sometimes been very detrimental to the well-being of clergy."[12]

In short it isn't easy being a pastor in today's world. This is something that your pastor may not communicate to you. Yet it is something that church people need to know. What is it exactly about church ministry that makes the pastor's job so stressful? Let's examine some factors. [13]

THE PASTOR'S WORK IS NEVER DONE

A pastor has no set schedule. He cannot punch out, go home and forget about his work. He is always on call – night and day, 24/7. Every pastor can tell stories of phone calls that interrupted a good night's sleep, important family time, or a much needed vacation. The advent of cell phones has only made this more of a problem.

When the call is a genuine life-or-death emergency, then it is acceptable. I welcome calls concerning an automobile accident or a life-threatening heart attack. The pastor is legitimately on call to provide pastoral care at such times. But too often the "emergency" is a long-standing personal problem or church issue that could have waited until the next day. I used to have a sign in my office that read "Lack of planning on your part does not constitute an emergency on my part." That pastoral advice was only imperfectly heeded.

Even on a normal day it is not unusual for a pastor to receive telephone calls late into the evening. Often the request is prefaced by the words, "Pastor, I know it is late, but…." or "I know it is your day off, but…." I have always felt like replying, "If you know it is my day off, why the heck are you calling?!" But of course I never said that. A pastor has to be nice and polite, no matter how inconsiderate people might be.

The never-ending work week of the pastor can create havoc with the pastor's health, marriage, and family relationships. A pastor's spouse and children have a right to have the pastor's undivided attention at times. A 12 year-old's birthday party is more important than a church budget meeting. The pastor needs to set an example for her parishioners by putting her family first, even when it means that some church business is left undone. As the minister's variation on the old saying goes: "No one ever said on his deathbed, 'I wish I had spent more time at the church.'"

The problem is that the "all-or-nothing, all-consuming, eternally important" rhetoric surrounding the spiritual life lends itself to unhealthy self-sacrificial behavior. A person's eternal soul might be at stake! How can I say "No?" The inability to say "No" to church people and church activities can cause serious problems for a pastor. It is a recipe for burnout, depression, divorce, or suicide.

THE PASTOR HAS NO CLEAR STANDARDS FOR SUCCESS

How does one judge the success of a pastor's ministry? In our statistic-obsessed culture often the only measure of success is the bottom line – how many people are in the pews and how many dollars are in the plates. Attendance and giving are often the only standards by which pastors can measure their success or failure in ministry.

I remember attending a Church Growth conference many years ago. My roommate was a young pastor who spent his free time in our hotel room endlessly going over the worship attendance figures for this congregation. He appeared to be on the verge of a nervous breakdown. It was clear to me that his sense of self-worth was tied to numbers. It was all I could do not to knock him on the side of the head and tell him to stop worrying. He was making me anxious just listening to him!

Unfortunately all the statistics show that every denomination is declining these days. Some mainline Protestant denominations – such as the Episcopal Church and the Presbyterian Church USA - are in freefall. But the downward trend is affecting even conservative denominations. Recent figures have shown that Southern Baptists, who measure their faithfulness to the gospel by the number of baptisms, are in decline. Both the number of baptisms and church attendance for the Southern Baptist Convention have been going down for a decade.

American society is becoming more secular. Those who claim no religious affiliation are growing with each successive generation. The trend is accelerating, and there is no end in sight. Atheism and agnosticism are growing. Short of a nationwide religious revival, the United States is going the way of Great Britain and Western Europe, where religious faith is an oddity.

Congregational growth is the exception in American Christianity. Where it exists at all, it is in new church startups and megachurches, which can offer potential members a wide variety of programs for the whole family. How can the pastor of an average church compete? The average church in the US has less than 100 people in attendance on the weekend, according to a 2016 study from the Hartford Institute for Religious Research. The median size of church membership is 75.

A rising tide lifts all boats, as the saying goes. Unfortunately that means that a falling tide lowers them. The tide is going out on American Christianity in the twenty-first century, and there is nothing your pastor can do to stem the tide.

The hard truth, which your pastor will not tell you, is that your church is declining. It will likely continue to decline regardless of how gifted, dedicated, and hard-working your pastor is. I can hear the groans of my clergy colleagues now, "That is lack of faith and defeatism. Think positive! Nothing is impossible with God!" True, nothing is impossible, but some things are highly improbable.

What I am saying is not pessimism or lack of faith; it is reality. Whether or not we accept it, it is the new normal. Of course there are exceptions. You might be able to point to a church in your area that is beating the odds and growing. But that church is probably growing at the expense of other churches – people transferring from dying churches to vibrant ones.

Some churches truly beat the odds and grow dramatically, but those are few and far between. They are the exceptions. Somebody has to win the lottery; that is the nature of lotteries. But the odds are not good that it will be your church.

Unless your pastor is judged by the congregation – and judges herself – by a different standard than church growth, her ministry is doomed to failure. Your church will decline even faster with a disheartened pastor and a discouraged congregation.

So what is a realistic standard of success for a pastor? That is just the problem; there isn't one. Once one abandons numerical growth as a feasible measure of success, one is left with very vague alternatives. None of them can be easily measured. How does one measure a congregation's spiritual growth and maturity? How does one judge faithfulness to God and Christ?

You could count the number of meals served to the homeless or visits to the elderly. But that could also lead to burnout if annual growth in these numbers are the criterion of success. It is well-known church maxim that 80% of the work is done by 20% of the people. As that 20% ages and declines, the number of programs and activities done by a church also declines.

There is no clear standard of success for a pastor. So he is often left to his feelings or the feelings of those in his congregation. Feelings are fickle. On a good Sunday we might feel up, and on a bad Sunday down. That is no way to judge Christian ministry. The fact is that the lack of a clear standard for success in ministry is problematic for the mental, emotional, and spiritual health of a pastor – and a church.

SOME OF THE PASTOR'S JOB CAN BE DONE BY OTHERS IN THE CHURCH

The pastor has a lot on his plate. More than he has time to do. To maximize his time and talents, some of what a pastor is expected to do can be more effectively done by laypeople in the church.

Let me make this clear. Much of what the pastor does in ministry is best done only by the pastor. This would involve those things for which he was trained in seminary. The interpretation and proclamation of the Bible and Christian theology are best done by those who have extensively studied the Bible and Christian theology.

The same is true of spiritual direction and counseling. Only those trained in pastoral counseling should undertake the care of souls. If lay people have received this training, then that is fine. But if not, then it should be left to the pastor.

Church administration is another area that the pastor has expertise. It is no easy feat to keep a volunteer organization like a church moving forward, navigating the rough waters of conflict resolution and organizational dead ends. My experience is that a church without a pastor is like a ship without a rudder. It is amazing what unnecessary trouble a church can get itself into when it does not have someone at the helm. It tends to be like a ship "tossed to and fro by the waves and carried about by every wind of doctrine, by human cunning, by craftiness in deceitful schemes." (Ephesians 4:14)

But many of the other things that the pastor does can easily be done – and often done better – by the laypeople in the congregation. To pay the pastor to do what can be done by volunteers is a waste of the pastor's time and the church's money.

Here is one example. This is a story told to me years ago by a pastor in the north country of New Hampshire. A small church had called him as their new pastor during the summer. He was fresh out of seminary, and all things were moving along smoothly, as they often do during the so-called "honeymoon period." One Sunday morning in September the pastor arrived at the church a bit early, as he always did. It had been a particularly cold Saturday night, and when he got to church the sanctuary was freezing!

After a few minutes one of the deacons arrived at the church, and he also immediately noticed the cold. "Why isn't there any heat in here?" he demanded of the pastor. "I don't know," the minister replied. "I just got here, and it was like this when I arrived." The deacon answered, "Why didn't you get here early and start the woodstove? That is the pastor's job, you know!"

The previous pastor had always gotten up early on Sundays, come to the church and started a fire in the woodstove. But no one had thought to inform the new pastor that this was part of his job description. They just assumed that fire-building was the pastor's responsibility.

Every pastor does things that are not in her formal contract. Some of it involves the upkeep and maintenance of the building. How many times have I shoveled snow, put sand on icy steps, made sure the furnace or air conditioning is on, opened and closed windows, locked and unlocked doors, go to the church to turn off lights in the middle of the night, and many other chores?

Some of it is understandable. It is just part of being part of a congregation. Many churches have a self-appointed handyman, who does all sorts of odd jobs around the church. They are the pastor's greatest blessing. Everybody chips in when there is a need, including the pastor ... even if it is not in his job description.

If I am leading a Bible Study or attending a meeting at the church, I think nothing of setting up chairs and tables. Anybody would do the same. But there are other things that should not be the pastor's responsibility, like arriving in the dark hours of Sunday morning to light the woodstove, or mowing the church's lawn, or opening the church for the local AA meeting. That can be done by others.

Likewise much of the visitation load can be shared by laypeople in the congregation. Some types of visits the pastor needs to do, such as emergency hospital calls, funeral preparation meetings, wedding planning, etc. But many times all a person needs is a friendly face. This is especially true of the elderly and the homebound. It is also true of many other types of visits. Deacons or a Visitation Committee in the church can do such visits just as well as the pastor. These visits are often more appreciated by those who receive them because – unlike the pastor – they aren't getting paid to do it.

I was trained "old school." I believe it is important for the pastor to be visiting his parishioners in their homes on a regular basis, even when there is no urgent need. This is especially true of first time visitors to a worship service. A timely phone call and/or visit by the pastor communicates Christian love. The same is true of hospital visits. The crisis of life-threatening illness is best addressed by someone who is experienced, trained and comfortable talking about life-or-death issues.

But other people in the church can have visitation as their ministry. Studies have shown that speaking to a friend is just as effective in resolving emotional problems as speaking to a professional counselor or clergy member. Most people just need to know that someone cares. All they want is for someone to listen to them. You don't have to have any – or at least not much – training to listen.

Committee meetings are another area where laypeople can take the lead. I have a confession to make. I hate committee meetings. When I was a full-time pastor, endless meetings seemed to fill my evenings, often stretching my workdays into 12 hour days. I would have rather been reading my children a bedtime story.

One of the best things I love about retirement is that I do not have to attend meetings! As a pastor I attended almost every meeting in the church because I am a hands-on, micro-management, type of guy. The truth is it would have been better for the church if I had stepped back a bit and oversaw the work of the committees from a distance.

A story from the life of Moses teaches this. It is found in Exodus 18:13-26. Moses was busy "from morning to evening" judging cases for his people. The story says, "When Moses' father-in-law saw all that he was doing for the people, he said, 'What is this that you are doing for the people? Why do you sit alone, and all the people stand around you from morning till evening?'"

Jethro knew this was a formula for burnout. Jethro's advice was for Moses to get help. He said, "Moreover, look for able men from all the people, men who fear God, who are trustworthy and hate a bribe, and place such men over the people as chiefs of thousands, of hundreds, of fifties, and of tens. And let them judge the people at all times. Every great matter they shall bring to you, but any small matter they shall decide themselves. So it will be easier for you, and they will bear the burden with you. If you do this, God will direct you, you will be able to endure, and all this people also will go to their place in peace."

Jethro taught Moses to delegate authority and responsibility. And it worked. "So Moses listened to the voice of his father-in-law and did all that he had said. Moses chose able men out of all Israel and made them heads over the people, chiefs of thousands, of hundreds, of fifties, and of tens. And they judged the people at all times. Any hard case they brought to Moses, but any small matter they decided themselves."

A pastor does not have to do it all. She just needs to oversee it all. That is actually the definition of one of the biblical words for the pastor, episkopos (ἐπίσκοπος), which means overseer. It is actually better for both the pastor and her congregation if she shares responsibility for ministry. That is something that I wished I had learned, and had the courage to do, earlier in my ministry. The pastor's job is not to do all the work of ministry, but "to equip the saints for the work of ministry, for building up the body of Christ." (Ephesians 4:12)

Your pastor is not the church's employee, regardless of what church's ruling board thinks. It does not even say that on a pastor's tax forms! According to the IRS a pastor is self-employed. According to Scripture he is God-employed. The pastor is not at the church's beck and call. He is at Christ's beck and call. Paul's favorite title for himself is "bondservant of Christ." The pastor is not the church's servant; he is the servant of Christ. You are fellow servants with him, doing the work of ministry together as a church. If we can get this concept of servanthood through our heads, then much of the misunderstandings and frustrations concerning the pastor's ministry is resolved.

THE PASTOR'S WORK IS EMOTIONALLY DRAINING

The African American spiritual says: "Nobody knows the trouble I've seen. Nobody knows my sorrow. Nobody knows the trouble I've seen. Nobody knows but Jesus." If there is one thing I wish I could communicate to every church, it is the traumatic nature of the ministry. Most people deal with major crises a few times in their lives. Pastors deal with them every day.

The death of a loved one is traumatic for a family. A pastor deals with death every week.

Constantly someone in his church that he knows (and loves) has died or is dying. A pastor – especially these days – does many more funerals than weddings or baptisms. Furthermore funeral preparations are more stretched out. It used to be that a person died, and the funeral was held within a week. Now the process is stretched out over months, as memorial services are postponed to fit family schedules and weather conditions.

As churches gray, a higher percentage of people in the church are chronically and terminally ill. Church members do not realize the toll this takes on the pastor. The pastor is not like a funeral director, who usually deals with people they do not know. Pastors suffer with (the literal meaning of sympathize) our church members. These are our friends.

I served a community church in New Hampshire for 12 years in the 1980's and early 90's. Then I moved on to other churches in other states. I returned to the same congregation in New Hampshire in 2011 to serve as their pastor for five more years before I retired in 2016. I have known many of the people in this congregation for well over thirty years. I saw their children and their grandchildren born. I baptized and married them. I love them deeply. For the last five years of my ministry I have buried them, and I am still burying them. Each funeral is like losing a member of my family.

As a pastor I am invited into the pain and suffering of a family like few other people. We cry at a person's deathbed. We mourn a serious medical diagnosis. We grieve during the dying process. Being a pastor hurts. That is something your pastor probably does not tell you.

Then there is another kind of pain. There is the pain of criticism and rejection. If a congregation is like a pastor's family, then conflict with a church member or losing a member can feel like divorce or like a child becoming estranged. Nothing hurts pastors like criticism, especially when they are trying their best. The reality is that criticism and rejection is inevitable. A pastor has to develop thick skin to survive in the ministry. Unfortunately – or perhaps it is fortunately – I never developed the emotional calluses necessary to make ministry easier.

Henri Nouwen coined the term "wounded healer" to describe this type of minister. In his classic book by that name, Nouwen explores how woundedness can become a source of strength and healing. He advises ministers – ordained and lay – to connect to the suffering of those around us and make that pain the power of our ministry. This is what it means, according to him, to pick up and carry the cross of Christ. This is bearing the image of Christ, who was "a man of sorrows and acquainted with grief." This small but powerful book, which I discovered in seminary, has been an inspiration for me for over forty years.

But ministry still hurts! And there are few places that a pastor can turn to deal with the pain. Studies have shown that pastors have few or no friends in the church that he or she can confide in. Nor do they have close friends outside the church. Pastoral Relations committees are designed to be a sounding board and a support for pastors. But too often they devolve into complaint committees that exacerbate the problems rather than alleviate them.

Denominations do little to support the struggling pastor. Denominations are also struggling with dwindling staff and resources. Furthermore pastors hesitate to confide in those in positions of authority in the denominational structure because they know that their professional future is dependent upon their endorsement and recommendation. Therefore many pastors simply tough it out and go it alone, which is not a healthy option.

I have been blessed to have access to professional counseling at various points during my ministry, and I used it. That is also something that pastors may not tell you. There is the myth prevalent in Christian circles that if a person is spiritually strong enough then they do not need counseling. "All you need is faith to get you through. Just trust in the Lord, and you will be alright." That advice is a lie from the depths of hell, and following that advice may send you spiraling into your own personal hell.

Pastors need a pastor. The counselor needs counseling. They need mental health care from a pastoral counselor, psychologist or psychiatrist, just like everyone else. Mental health is a problem for pastors, and they sometimes need professional help. There is no shame in it. In fact a pastor can be a model to his congregation by seeking professional mental healthcare.

On the first occasion I sought professional help I was blessed to have unlimited pastoral counseling provided free of charge by the Methodist conference. It was a godsend! Since that time, whenever I have felt the need, I have sought help. I have found it is often paid for – in whole or part - by health insurance. If not, many counselors will give clergy a discount. A psychology professor at a local Christian college provided counseling to me free. Denominations will often have special funds available to alleviate the cost.

There are things that a pastor can do, and a congregation can insist that their pastor do, to make it less likely it gets to the point of needing professional care. There are retreats and retreat centers available, often at little or no cost to the pastor. There are also specialized ministries that minister to pastors and their spouses who are going through difficult times. Twice I attended intensive retreats sponsored by SonScape Retreats based in Colorado. I credit it with saving my ministry.

There are less structured opportunities as well. A Christian camp near me has a cabin available free of charge for pastors and spouses to get away into the woods for a time of relaxation. Every part of the country has such ministries to pastors and their families. Both pastors and church would do well to seek them out and utilize them.

In addition I entered a program of spiritual direction. I received training as a spiritual director at the Shalem Institute in Washington, DC. As part of the training I had to be in spiritual direction. For many years I had a spiritual director that I met with regularly. A spiritual director is very different than a pastoral counselor, but the effect on the pastor's emotional – as well as spiritual – wellbeing is equally beneficial.

THE PASTOR DEALS WITH DYSFUNCTIONAL PEOPLE

Now I need to address the ugly underbelly of church life. Church is supposed to be a safe place. It is supposed to be a family of spiritual brothers and sisters who love one another with the self-sacrificial love of Christ. The reality is that the church sometimes harbors evil. It can harbor child abusers who prey on the most vulnerable members of a congregation.

The pedophile priest scandal of the Roman Catholic Church is well known. What is not as well known is that it is mirrored in Protestant and Evangelical churches. I had to personally confront a perpetrator and turn him over to the authorities. To be quite honest, it is the one time I think I could have killed someone. I was that angry and outraged. I am grateful that I did not own a handgun. I might have used it.

The #MeToo Movement that began in Hollywood has come to Protestant and Evangelical churches as ministers in positions of authority in churches, seminaries, and denominations have been exposed as criminals who have assaulted women throughout their careers. It even has its own hashtag: #ChurchToo. Not a week goes by that I do not read in the local or national news of some minister being accused or arrested.

In a revealing article in the *Christian Science Monitor*, Basyle Tchividjian, a grandson of evangelist Billy Graham and a law professor at Liberty University in Lynchburg, VA, describes his work as a prosecutor, investigating charges of sexual misconduct and child abuse for nearly three decades. Since the mid-2000's he has focused on churches, especially those within his own evangelical tradition. He has handled hundreds of cases over the years.

In 2003 Tchividjian founded an organization called GRACE, or Godly Response to Abuse in the Christian Environment. He says, "In the early 2000s, when the tragedy of the Catholic Church was just starting to emerge, I'm thinking to myself, and sharing with others, 'my goodness, Protestants for the most part have no clue that this is as serious an issue in their own churches.'"[14]

It is hard enough to get people – especially young families – to attend church without raising the specter of sexual assault in our churches. But the truth is that it is happening here. It cannot be ignored. Furthermore it cannot be stopped unless it is honestly addressed. That is why it is so important to properly vet anyone in any church position that has access to vulnerable persons.

I know from personal experience that there have been dysfunctional people in every one of the five churches I have served. I do not think my experience is unique. I am quite certain it is true of every church, including yours. That is something that your pastor probably will not tell you. Some people do not commit crimes of sexual assault, but they can still cause much harm to church members, churches and pastors.

One type of dysfunctional person is what researchers label "clergy killers." In his book *Clergy Killers,* pastoral counselor G. Lloyd Rediger calls them terrorists. He warns, "We are not just talking about conflict anymore, we are talking about emotional and spiritual abuse of traumatic proportions. And we are discovering that such abuse is exhausting pastors and draining the energy and resources of congregations and denominational programs."[15]

In his book *The Wounded Minister,* seminary professor and pastor Guy Greenfield also calls them "clergy killers," but he also has some other names for them: "pathological antagonists" and "well-intentioned dragons." He describes them as "troublesome persons who are emotionally and/or mentally disturbed."[16]

I am the victim of a clergy killer, who was also a member of the clergy. It sent me spiraling into depression. As a result I left ministry for a year and only returned due to the excellent care that I received. I will not get into the details of my personal life, but I raise the issue so that churches can be on the lookout for clergy killers in their midst. In talking to colleagues, my experience is not as rare as one might think.

I am not talking about normal run-of-the-mill complainers and critics in the church. That comes with the job of being a pastor of a congregation, where everyone in the church expects the pastor to live up to their expectations, even if they conflict with others' expectations. It is hard to have a hundred bosses!

Sometimes criticisms of a pastor are valid, and sometimes they are not. In either case they can usually be handled by face-to-face discussions or through the proper channels in a congregation or denomination. Sometimes the criticisms are not valid. Churches tends to attract people with emotional issues who act them out in the life of the congregation. I am not talking about either of these. I am talking about something much more serious.

Some churches have people with their own personal demons, who see it as their mission to destroy the pastor. It may be a retired pastor in the congregation who is the clergy killer, as it was in my case. It may be the chairman of the trustees or deacons. It is always someone who has power – either official or unofficial – and uses it to abuse the pastor. This is clergy abuse. It is emotional and verbal abuse. It needs to be confronted as vigorously as sexual or physical abuse.

I have found church and denominational structures to be inadequate to address the issue of clergy abuse. Pastoral Relations committees tend to treat it lightly; they do not understand the seriousness of the situation. Like the people of Jeremiah's day, "They have healed the wound of my people lightly, saying, 'Peace, peace,' when there is no peace." (Jeremiah 6:14) They do not want to confront powerful members of the congregation. It is easier to find a new pastor than to find new church members, especially if the members are generous and active.

Denominations tend to avoid the issue. In my case I took my case to the denominational committee responsible for addressing violations of the ministerial code of ethics, of which this was clearly a case. Repeated requests to present the facts went ignored, even though I had recently been on the Executive Committee of the region. The denominational executive made one phone call to the abuser, but backed down when he continued the abuse.

It became clear to me that the denomination was more interested in churches than pastors. Churches are hard to replace; pastors come and go. I found out the hard way that pastors are expendable. Pastors become the unfortunate, but inevitable, collateral damage in the battle to keep churches happy and contributing to the denomination.

This is not necessarily true of all denominations or even of all regions of my denomination. I have had an excellent relationship with every other region of my denomination. To be fair, my particular region was in a time of transition in its structure and leadership. But that is no excuse for turning a blind eye to abuse of any kind. The Roman Catholic Church has learned that the hard way, when bishops routinely turned a blind eye to abuse happening under their noses.

All churches have dysfunctional people, and pastors have to deal with them. Some churches have abusers in them, and pastors have to deal with them as well. Some churches have clergy killers in them. The pastor cannot handle these by himself, for he is the victim in this case. Pastors need help from church and denominational leaders. Although I have no interest in starting a #PastorsToo Movement (I don't even have a Twitter account), this is something all churches need to know, even though your pastor won't tell you.

2

WHAT YOUR PASTOR WON'T TELL YOU ABOUT THE BIBLE

The previous section likely produced some "Amens" from pastors and other Christians involved in ministry. It addressed the type of issues that Christians anywhere on the theological spectrum can appreciate. This section may not resonate with as broad an audience. It deals with the content, nature, inspiration, and authority of Scripture. Christians – especially pastors – can get their undies in a bunch when someone starts saying things about the Bible that they disagree with. In spite of the risk of uncomfortable ecclesiastical bottoms I will dive right in. I will start with my least controversial statement.

MOST OF THE BIBLE IS NEVER READ IN CHURCHES

Pastors read scripture lessons in the worship service. They preach from a scripture passage. But most of the Bible is never read or preached in church. The Bible that is read in churches is an abridged version of the Scriptures, carefully edited and sanitized of uncomfortable portions. The Bible that is read in worship does not contain passages that the pastor does not want her congregation to know about. Why? Some parts of the Bible are just boring. Like the genealogies or the Leviticus holiness laws. Christian pastors never preach from Leviticus – unless they are condemning homosexuality.

Other Bible verses are downright hateful. The Bible is an X-rated book unfit for a G-rated church. How many sermons have you heard on Psalm 137:9? "Blessed shall he be who takes your little ones and dashes them against the rock!" Chances are your pastor has never told you about that verse! Or how about Jesus' teaching on family values? "If anyone comes to me and does not hate his own father and mother and wife and children and brothers and sisters, yes, and even his own life, he cannot be my disciple." (Luke 14:26)

All pastors edit the Bible to fit their theology and ethics. They just don't tell you they are doing it. Preachers have a "canon within the canon." There are certain biblical books and passages that they preach from and others that they avoid. The ancient practice of using a lectionary in church was designed to correct this tendency of pastors to preach from only a small number of favorite passages.

All Catholics, Orthodox, and most Protestants follow the lectionary. A lectionary is a selection of readings from the Bible for use in public worship. The practice goes back to the fourth century. Think of it as the Reader's Digest Condensed Bible.

The Revised Common Lectionary is used by most Protestant denominations today. It has a three year cycle of readings from the Old and New Testaments. It contains only 13 percent of the Bible - 5 percent of the Old Testament and 41 percent of the New Testament. That means that 87% of the Bible (including more than half of the New Testament) is never read from Christian pulpits! If it is not read, you can be sure it is not preached! I bet your pastor never told you he only uses 13% of the Bible.

A couple of weeks ago I ran into a former church member in a store. He was telling me how he loves to hear the Old Testament read and preached in church. He was lamenting the fact that this happens so seldom these days. Even when the Old Testament is read as one of the lectionary readings, the preacher usually chooses to preach from the Gospel or Epistle Lesson instead. But he was comforted by the "fact" that the use of the lectionary ensures that the whole Bible is read in worship every three years. It was painful for him to hear from me the truth about the lectionary. The whole Bible is not read. Not even close.

Evangelical and Fundamentalist churches do not use the lectionary for that very reason. It too obviously skips over verses, chapters and whole books of the Bible. The lectionary also cramps their style. They prefer to rely on the Holy Spirit to choose their scripture text for them. To be forced to use a particular Bible passage on any particular Sunday is to "quench the Spirit." They are proud that they do not limit God or edit God's Word.

But the reality is that the percentage of the Bible read and preached in evangelical churches is even smaller than mainline and Catholic churches. Evangelical pastors have their favorite books and passages that they preach from over and over again. Whole books are never mentioned. When is the last time you heard a sermon on the Song of Solomon, Obadiah, or Jude?

Pastors will say that the entire Bible is the Word of God. Evangelical preachers are adamant that every word of the Bible is inspired by God. They even have a phrase for it: the verbal plenary inspiration of the Bible. But they do not preach the whole Bible. The reason is easy to discover when one actually reads the whole Bible for oneself.

The discipline of reading through the whole Bible in a year is advocated by many pastors and churches, although accomplished by only a small percentage of a congregation. I have led "Through the Bible in a Year" classes many times during my ministry. Inevitably the actual content of the Bible comes as a shock to those Christians who make it past the genealogies of Genesis, the laws of Exodus, and the purity code of Leviticus. There is a lot of offensive stuff in the Bible!

I will talk about the offensive parts of the Bible later. For now it is sufficient to point out that very little of the Bible is taught in church on Sunday morning. Even if your pastor uses the lectionary, he usually focuses on only one of the three lectionary readings for the day, meaning that your pastor has actually taught far less than 13% of the Bible.

There is no good reason for it. A seven year cycle of readings could include the whole New Testament. A twenty year cycle would include all of the Old Testament. Why not do it this way? Especially if we really believe that every verse of the Bible is the Word of God. We certainly have the time! If not, we should make the time – if we really believe these are inspired words from the Creator of the universe to us!

There are exceptions - pastors who preach the whole Bible. I had a friend who served a nearby church in New Hampshire. He took upon himself the task of preaching on every book in the Bible. He preached on a different book every Sunday. His plan was to preach all 66 books of the Bible in 66 Sundays. Excluding vacations and holidays, he figured it would take him about a year and a half to preach through the Bible.

He was asked to resign before he got through the Minor Prophets. The congregation admitted that the reason he was asked to leave was the content of his preaching. They said his preaching had become too judgmental. I wonder if they had ever read the Old Testament prophets! Lots of judgment there!

THE BIBLE CONTAINS ERRORS

The Bible has errors. Lots of them - scientific, historical, factual errors. Some of the errors are revealed as contradictions within the Bible. When different books of the Bible contradict each other concerning the same event, they can't both be right.

One – or both – of them has to have it wrong. Sometimes these contradictions are dramatic.

One example is the two accounts of David ordering a census of his people. It is found in the parallel accounts of 1 Chronicles 21:1–17 and 2 Samuel 24:1–25. First Chronicles 21:1-2 says, "Then Satan stood against Israel and incited David to number Israel. So David said to Joab and the commanders of the army, 'Go, number Israel, from Beersheba to Dan, and bring me a report, that I may know their number.'"

2 Samuel 24:1-2 says almost the same thing. "Again the anger of the Lord was kindled against Israel, and he incited David against them, saying, 'Go, number Israel and Judah.' So the king said to Joab, the commander of the army, who was with him, 'Go through all the tribes of Israel, from Dan to Beersheba, and number the people, that I may know the number of the people.'"

One says Satan ordered the census and the other says God. That is a big difference with serious consequences! Jesus identifies the sin of "blasphemy against the Holy Spirit" as not being able to distinguish between the work of God and the devil. (Matthew 12:22-32) Biblical apologists have come up with ingenuous ways to resolve this contradiction, but they all smack of sophistry. Short of saying that

God and Satan are two names for the same character (something Christians are loathe to do) there is no good resolution to this problem.

The simplest solution is to admit that the two different authors of these two different biblical books saw the inspiration of the census very differently. They simply disagreed. It is as simple as that! And why not? Authors disagree all the time. Only if we try to force the Bible into a preconceived mold of inerrancy is this a problem.

The most frequently noted contradictions in the Bible surround the central events of the New Testament – the death and resurrection of Jesus. The four canonical gospels disagree on many of the details of what happened on Good Friday and Easter morning. (For a complete analysis of the gospel accounts of the resurrection, see my book *The Evolution of Easter: How the Historical Jesus Became the Risen Christ*, 2018.)

Was Jesus crucified on the day before Passover, as the Gospel of John says (19:31) or the day after the Passover, as the other gospels attest? It can't be both. The solution is that John changed the date for theological purposes, in order to have Jesus die at exactly the time when the Passover Lambs were being slaughtered.

When Jesus died, did an earthquake open the graves of many saints, who later arose from the dead, walked around Jerusalem and were seen by many on Easter? Only Matthew reports this remarkable event. If it really happened it is hard to imagine other gospel writers omitting this dramatic event from their accounts of Easter day.

How many women came to the tomb on Easter morning? Was it one, as John says? Two, as Matthew says? Three, as Mark says? Or more, as Luke records? Was the stone already rolled away when the women arrived at the tomb, as Mark, Luke, and John say? Or did an angel come down and move the stone after they arrived, as Matthew says.

Who did the women see at the tomb? Were they angels or young men? Matthew and John say angels; Mark and Luke say men. Matthew and Mark say there was one. Luke and John say two.

Did the women tell the disciples what they had seen at the tomb? Mark says, "They said nothing to anyone, because they were afraid." (16:8) Matthew and Luke make clear that they told the disciples immediately.

Could Jesus's followers touch him? John says no; Matthew and Luke say yes. Where were the disciples instructed to go in order to meet the risen

Christ? Galilee (Matthew and Mark) or Jerusalem (Luke and Acts)?

How many days did Jesus appear to his disciples after his resurrection? Luke wrote in his gospel that Jesus ascended into heaven the same day as the resurrection (Luke 24:51). The Book of Acts, (traditionally said to be written by the same author) says that "He appeared to them over a period of forty days" (Acts 1:3).

There are many more differences between the four gospel accounts, but that is enough to make the point. The gospels contradict each other. Christian apologists go to great lengths to harmonize the four accounts, as if the integrity and reliability of the Scriptures rest upon coming up with some kind of feasible solution.

The most honest apologists will admit there are irreconcilable differences between the gospel accounts of the resurrection. They liken it to how four bystanders would report the details of a crime or an automobile accident that they had witnessed. They point out that the differences in details don't discredit the accuracy of the main facts of the case. In those essentials they all agree. So what if they got a few of the details wrong?

Exactly! That is my point! People make mistakes. They get details wrong. That is true of the people who wrote the gospels and the other books of the Bible. The Bible contains errors.

It not only has historical errors, it also has scientific errors, which one would expect from a book written thousands of years before the Scientific Revolution. The authors of the Bible were understandably ignorant of the fact that the earth was a sphere, that it revolves around the sun and not vice-versa, that the earth is 4.5 billion years old, and that all life on evolved from single-celled organisms over billions of years.

The Bible contains errors, and that is alright! There is nothing wrong with that. The Bible never claims to be without error. The Bible writers make some claims about the inspiration and reliability of Scripture, but none of them say that the Bible needs to be taken literally on all scientific and historical matters.

What does the Bible says about itself? The most quoted verses regarding the inspiration of Scripture is 2 Timothy 3:16-17. "All Scripture is inspired [breathed out] by God and profitable for teaching, for reproof, for correction, and for training in righteousness, that the man of God may be competent, equipped for every good work."

2 Peter 1:20-21 also speaks about how scripture was inspired. It says, "No prophecy of Scripture

WHAT YOUR PASTOR WON'T TELL YOU

comes from someone's own interpretation. For no prophecy was ever produced by the will of man, but men spoke from God as they were carried along by the Holy Spirit."

These passages say that the Scriptures – or at least the prophetic texts of Scripture - are inspired. They claim that in some way God was the source of what was considered to be Scripture at that time. Of course they are referring to the Old Testament. The New Testament was not in existence when these statements were made, so these claims do not apply to the Christian books of the New Testament. The apostle Paul would have been shocked to think his personal letters would be considered equal to the Torah.

There is one passage in the New Testament that refers to the letters of Paul in connection with scripture. The author of Second Peter, writing late in the first century, is aware of Paul's writings. He says, "Our beloved brother Paul also wrote to you according to the wisdom given him, as he does in all his letters when he speaks in them of these matters. There are some things in them that are hard to understand, which the ignorant and unstable twist to their own destruction, as they do the other Scriptures." (2 Peter 3:15-16)

Some interpret the reference to "other Scriptures" to mean that the author considered Paul's writings also to be Scripture. But probably not. The word translated "scripture" grapha (γραφή) means "writing" – any type of writing. We would need more evidence than this one verse to conclude that Paul's writings were seen as authoritative this early. Church history makes it clear that no New Testament books were considered Holy Scripture on the level with the Hebrew Scriptures until centuries later. So that is probably not what is meant here.[17]

When the New Testament speaks of Scripture it is talking about the Hebrew Scriptures, what Christians call the Old Testament, and not even all of that. At the time the New Testament was being written, the Hebrew Scriptures consisted only of the Law and the Prophets, not the Writings (books like Proverbs, Job, Esther, Ecclesiastes, etc.) Old Testament statements concerning the inspiration of Scripture, such as Psalm 19, ("The law of the Lord is perfect, reviving the soul; the testimony of the Lord is sure, making wise the simple;") refer only to the Law or Torah, which we call the Pentateuch, the first five books of the Old Testament.

The canon of the whole Bible was not decided until the fifth century. Even then the contents of the Biblical canon were not universally accepted. Jews, Samaritans, Orthodox, Catholic, and Protestants still have differing lists of canonical books. This does not even take into consideration "heretical" groups that existed in the early centuries of Church, which had their own Scriptures. Then there are modern groups like the Mormons, who would add more books, which they say are equally ancient, inspired, and authoritative.

In any case there is no mention in the Bible that any Scripture is inerrant or infallible. It simply says that Scripture is inspired by God, and we are left to discern what that means. Fortunately the author of Second Timothy goes on to tell us what he has in mind. It says that the inspiration of Scripture means that it is "profitable for teaching, for reproof, for correction, and for training in righteousness, that the man of God may be competent, equipped for every good work." (2 Timothy 3:16-17)

In other words Scripture is useful for practical spiritual purposes. In most Protestant denominations that is understood to mean that Scripture is reliable "regarding matters of faith and Christian practice." Even those who speak of the "infallibility" of the Bible will qualify it to mean "that the Bible is completely trustworthy as a guide to salvation and the life of faith and will not fail to accomplish its purpose." [18]

In short the Bible is not infallible or inerrant on other matters, such as history or science. It does not claim to be. Whether it is infallible in spiritual matters is another question. The Bible does not make that claim for itself either. It simply claims that Scripture is "profitable" for certain spiritual and ethical matters.

Pastors know that. Yet it is seldom mentioned by pastors. Why? Because the average Christian has not thought through what it means to say the Bible is inspired. Most Christians assume it means that the Bible is never wrong on any topic. Most pastors do not take the time to correct their parishioners' faulty understanding of the nature of scripture.

I am constantly amazed at the misconceptions that people have about the Bible. I have known Christians who use the Bible like a divination tool, as if it were a Christian version of the *I Ching* or Tarot cards. When looking for guidance they will plop the Bible open to a random location, and begin reading, firmly believing that the Holy Spirit guided them to that particular page.

The Bible is treated like a magical book that contains the answers to every question we could have. At worst it is turned into an idol. In some Christian traditions this divine book is gilded in gold, paraded around the sanctuary, and kissed. Pastors understandably hesitate to dethrone this golden calf by calling attention to its errors. It would be equivalent to saying that the emperor has no clothes.

Pastors hesitate to correct misconceptions about the inspiration and authority of Scripture because it might be seen as an attack on Scripture itself. Pastors are more interested in teaching what the Bible actually says and means.

MUCH OF THE BIBLE IS MYTH

The Bible contains myths. That does not mean it is not true. Myth is true. It is just not literally true. It is truth communicated through symbols. Tolkien said myth is "a symbolic interpretation of the beauties and terrors of the world." In his famous series of interviews with mythologist Joseph Campbell, Bill Moyers said, "Myths are stories of the search by men and women through the ages for meaning, for significance, to make life signify, to touch the eternal, to understand the mysterious, to find out who we are." To which Campbell added, "Myths are clues to the spiritual potentialities of the human life."[19]

I would define myths as true fictions. Myths are true, but not in a literal, historical, or scientific sense. They are true in a spiritual and symbolic sense. They are true insofar as they communicate spiritual and eternal truths. They are fictions insofar as they did not historically happen.

Many of the most well-known stories of the Bible did not really happen. There was no Garden of Eden, Tree of Life, Tree of Knowledge, Adam and Eve, Cain and Abel. There was probably no Abraham, Isaac, Jacob and Joseph. Possibly no Moses. If there were actual historical personages with those names, they were nothing like the larger-than-life figures of Genesis and Exodus. The world was not created in six days. There was no worldwide flood, no Exodus from Egypt, or wilderness wandering. Scientific and archeological evidence confirms that these things never happened.

Let's take the Garden of Eden as an example. It should be clear to the modern reader that when we have stories about talking serpents and magical trees that we are in the realm of myth, not history. It is the stuff of Aesop's Fables, not the Evening News. Yet in a 2014 Gallup poll 56% said they believed Adam and Eve were real people. The poll goes on to reveal that 51 percent believe that the Bible is without error.[20]

Do these people believe that somewhere on earth today in the Middle East there is a seraph with a flaming sword guarding the Tree of Life to prevent people from eating of it and living forever, just like Genesis says? If so, where is it? Was it relocated? Did the Tree of Life die?

It should be obvious that the early chapters of Genesis are symbolic. This would include the biblical Creation accounts. It is frequently pointed out that there are two creation accounts in the first two chapters of Genesis. There are actually over 20 creation accounts in the Bible,[21] including at least one that refers to the creation myth popular throughout the ancient Near East about a primordial sea monster slain by God as part of the creative process. (Psalm 74)

The first chapter of Genesis says that the sun, moon and stars were created after the earth. Genesis 2 has all other animal life created after humans. Scientifically speaking this is nonsense. Not only do the two Genesis accounts disagree with scientific discoveries, they disagree with each other about the order in which things were created. In Genesis 1 humans were created last, after all the animals. In Genesis 2 humans were created first, before the animals. If we take the sequence in both accounts literally they can't both be true. One or both must be in error.

It seems obvious that the final editor of Genesis took two creation stories circulating at the time (in the sixth century BC) and included them both in Genesis. He knew that they disagreed in details, but they both had something important to say. The disagreements between the two did not bother him one bit! In fact the placement of two contradictory stories side by side would have indicated to the careful reader that he should not take either one literally. If God inspired both of these accounts, then it means that God was trying to tell us not to take them literally!

If we take the creation myths symbolically there is no problem. If they are understood to be communicating theology and not history, then they make perfect sense. They each have a theological reason for the placement of the creation of humans. Both in their own way were describing humans as the crowning achievement of God. In one humans are the first-born of creation. In the other they are the culmination of God's good creation.

Two leading British evangelical Christians have convincingly made the case that allegorical and symbolic interpretations of the creation stories were the normative way that Genesis was understood throughout the history of Christianity until recent centuries. The literalist approach came much later. They write: "There is, unfortunately, a common misconception that Christians all used to take it [Creation] fairly literally, and that in a post-Copernican and Darwinian age some of us are now trying to cobble together some kind of non-literal understanding. This is simply not true. At no stage in the history of Christian interpretation of Genesis 1 – 3 has there been a 'purely literal' understanding."[22]

What is true of the creation myths is also true of other fantastical stories in the Bible, such as the building of the tower of Babel that reached heaven, a worldwide flood, Noah's ark that housed every type of animal on earth, Joshua causing the sun and moon to stand still, Balaam's donkey speaking, and Jonah and his "big fish."

We are given many hints throughout the Book of Jonah that the "whale" ought to be taken symbolically. When Jonah prays in the belly of the fish (chapter 2) he describes himself as "in the belly of Sheol," which is the Hebrew abode of the dead. Jesus (or at least the author of the Gospel of Matthew) clearly takes it that way, seeing it as symbolic of Jesus' own death. (Matthew 12:40)

Later in the story when Jonah preaches to Nineveh, not only do all the Assyrians repent and don sackcloth, so do all the animals! That must have been quite a sight! That ought to be a hint to the reader that the author intends us not to take the actions of animals in the story too literally. In short the Bible is filled with mythical stories that are not intended to be taken literally. To do so is to badly misunderstand them.

The Bible Contains Forgeries

Forgery is a strong word. Biblical scholars prefer to call them "pseudonymous works," which is just a nicer term for forgeries. Your pastor will probably never mention that the Bible includes forgeries, even though it is well-known. That is because the idea of forgery carries with it a sense of illegitimacy. No pastor wants to be seen calling into question the legitimacy of the Bible. But the fact remains that it is well-established in biblical scholarship that many of the books of the Bible were not written by the people named in their titles.

Only the most conservative traditionalists believe that Moses wrote the Pentateuch, the first five books of the Old Testament, traditionally referred to as the "books of Moses." Nowhere do those books say they were penned by Moses. In fact the book of Deuteronomy records the death and burial of Moses, which is something very difficult for even a divinely inspired Moses to do.

Biblical scholars have identified at least five different strata of written sources in the Pentateuch, all of which are dated much later than Moses. This theory of Pentateuchal development is called the Documentary Hypothesis and is routinely taught in seminary and divinity school. It is often referred to simply as JEDP, which refers to four "authors" whose works have been identified in the Hebrew Scriptures: the Yahwist, Elohist, Deuteronomist, and Priestly source. The earliest of these is the J source, which is dated to the tenth or ninth century BC. That would place him three to five hundred years after Moses, depending on when you date the historical Moses.

Many Old Testament books do not pretend to be written by the Biblical characters that bear their names: books like Joshua, Ruth, and First and Second Samuel. Ecclesiastes and Song of Solomon are attributed to King Solomon, but no serous scholar takes those claims seriously. The same is true of Job.

In the New Testament we have a somewhat different situation. The four gospels are anonymous works. The authors are not mentioned in the text, and the names of Matthew, Mark, Luke, and John were added to the books in the second century. There is no reason to think that they were written by these apostles or apostolic companions.

In fact in the final verses of the Gospel of John (21:24-25), the author of the gospel refers to himself in the first person ("I") thereby distinguishing himself from John, whom he refers to in the third person as "he" in these final verses and the "beloved disciple" throughout the gospel. The author also refers to the spiritual community out of which the gospel came as "we." But he also says that this gospel is based on the written testimony of this beloved disciple. By its own testimony this gospel was a collective work, written by an anonymous representative of the Johannine community.

When we come to the epistles of Paul, we have biblical evidence that there were forgeries circulating in his name. Second Thessalonians refers to them. "Now concerning the coming of our Lord Jesus Christ and our being gathered together to him, we ask you, brothers, not to be quickly shaken in mind or alarmed, either by a spirit or a spoken word, or *a letter seeming to be from us*, to the effect that the day of the Lord has come. Let no one deceive you in any way." (2 Thessalonians 2:1-3)

Forgeries in the names of apostles were commonplace in the early Christian centuries. We have many of them. In 1945 a cache of such works, known as the Nag Hammadi library, was discovered in Upper Egypt. The importance of this find for the study of early Christianity is greater than the famous Dead Sea Scrolls, which included no Christian works.

We have non-canonical works from Nag Hammadi and elsewhere attributed to Thomas, Phillip, Peter, Mary Magdalene, Paul, Silvanus, Seth, Melchizedek, Judas, Barnabas, and many others. No one believes that they were actually written by the people to whom they are attributed.

When we come to the works that made it into the New Testament, people are more hesitant to claim they are outright forgeries. But it is the consensus of New Testament scholars that several of the letters of Paul in the New Testament were not actually written by him. Of the letters attributed to Paul only seven letters are accepted as authentic: Romans, 1 & 2 Corinthians, Galatians, Philippians, 1 Thessalonians, and Philemon. Three others are doubtful: Ephesians, Colossians, 2 Thessalonians. Three are certainly not written by Paul. These are known as the Pastoral Epistles: 1 & 2 Timothy and Titus. This is the consensus of mainstream biblical scholarship.

In addition to that, it is widely believed that 1 & 2 Peter were not written by the apostle Peter. The Letter of James does not claim to be written by the apostle James, although it is often attributed to him. He only refers to himself as "James, a servant of God and of the Lord Jesus Christ." (1:1) The name James was as common then as it is now, and this James does not claim to be the brother of Jesus.

The same is true of the Book of Revelation, whose author only identifies himself as "I, John, your brother and partner in the tribulation and the kingdom and the patient endurance that are in Jesus." (1:9) But this book is also traditionally attributed to the apostle John. The little Letter of Jude likewise is unclear as to its authorship, although it is generally believed that the author intends to pass himself off as the brother of Jesus and the apostle James. In that case this would also be a pseudonymous work.

In short there are lots of forgeries in the Bible, which your pastor probably never told you about. These do not discredit the usefulness of these works in advancing the spiritual life of the church. It does not necessarily mean that they were not "inspired by God" and "profitable for teaching, for reproof, for correction, and for training in righteousness, that the man of God may be competent, equipped for every good work." (2 Timothy 3:16-17)

But it does mean that pastors need to be forthright about the nature and authorship of the Bible, if the church's ministry is to be based on truth and honesty. And it should cause us to rethink the inspiration of Scripture. What does it mean to say that God inspired forgeries, when he could have just as easily inspired real apostles to write his Bible?

MANY BOOKS WERE LEFT OUT OF THE BIBLE

The Bible did not magically fall from heaven in its present form. The Bible has a long, convoluted and contested history. Some books just barely made it into the Bible – books like Hebrews, James, 2 Peter, 2 and 3 John, and Revelation. Other books that were widely accepted as scripture by the early Christians did not make the cut. These are books such as Third Corinthians, the Letter of Barnabas, 1 & 2 Clement, Shepherd of Hermas, Apocalypse of Peter, and the Didache, also known as the Teaching of the Twelve Apostles. All of these are known to have been used as Scripture in churches, according to the writings of the early Church Fathers.

The ancient Bible manuscripts known as the "four great uncial codices" are the earliest extant copies of the Greek Old and New Testament in existence. Their contents are good indications of the state of the Christian canon at the time they were produced. None of them contain the same books as the Bible on your bookshelf. That is true even if we limit our investigation to New Testament books.

The oldest copy of the Bible is Codex Vaticanus, dated c. 325–350 AD. It does not contain 1 and 2 Timothy, Titus, Philemon, and Revelation. The next oldest is Codex Sinaiticus, written c. 330–360. It has all our present books, but also includes the Epistle of Barnabas and The Shepherd of Hermas as part of the New Testament. Codex Alexandrinus, c. 400–440, includes 1 and 2 Clement in the New Testament. Codex Ephraemi Rescriptus, dated 450 AD, excludes 2 Thessalonians and 2 John. All the evidence we have points to the fact that the canon was still flexible even in the mid fifth century.

In addition to the books found in ancient copies of the Bible, there were lots of other gospels, letters, and apocalypses that did not have a chance of getting into the New Testament, because their teachings deviated from the "orthodox view." When the canon was closed, these texts were deemed heretical and were ordered destroyed. Only by the providence of God did some of them survive, like those found at Nag Hammadi. Most other works are lost to history, only known by their titles and quotations found in the works of the early Church Fathers.

Our Bible is a collection of books chosen by the ecclesiastical winners of a theological battle that raged for three hundred years. For three centuries Mediterranean Christianity was very diverse, with different scriptures used by different Christian communities. What we now know as orthodox Christianity – with its carefully defined doctrines of the Trinity and the Incarnation - won the theological war against groups now known as the Gnostics, Ebionites, Marcionites and many others. All these groups considered themselves Christians, but they were classified as heretics by their opponents.

The books of our New Testament teach orthodox Christian doctrine because the books that did not teach it were excluded from the canon and banned from use in the churches. This final censorship began in the fourth century when the newly converted emperor Constantine wanted a uniform Christianity to be the state religion. This required a unified theology and an established canon of scripture. It took a while for an exact list of biblical books to be completely accepted. But in the fifth century the process of canonization of scripture in the Western church was more or less completed.

The point is that the list of 66 books in the Bible – especially the 27 New Testament books – did not magically fall out of heaven. It was decided by humans who were fighting each other over correct theology, ecclesiology and ethics – just as churches do today. The Bible is the product of power struggles in the church and between bishops. It had a lot to do with Roman politics and an emperor who desired to unify his empire and consolidate his power through the imposition of a controversial new religion.

Those books used by minority Christian groups were excluded from the canon because they did not agree with the theology of the victorious majority. These books were banned, burned or buried. At best they sat neglected on the shelves of desert monasteries until rediscovered centuries later. Our knowledge of early Christianity is poorer today because of the loss of these books..

3

WHAT YOUR PASTOR WON'T TELL YOU ABOUT CHRISTIANITY & SCIENCE

Science is one of the greatest blessings of our age. It is single-handedly responsible for wiping out many deadly diseases, drastically reducing infant mortality, doubling the average human's life span, and preventing famine through modern agricultural techniques and hybrids. It has lifted us off this planet into space. It has given us a glimpse into the farthest reaches of the universe and back to the beginning of time. It has given us instant worldwide communication and placed encyclopedic knowledge at our fingertips.

You would think that such an extraordinary force for good, knowledge and truth would be embraced by the Church. But that has not been the case. In fact it has been just the opposite. There has been an ongoing war between science and religion. Instead of welcoming scientific discoveries as insights into the workings of God's creation, they have been seen as threats to God's revealed truths.

Among the major world's religions, Christianity in particular has historically held a hostile attitude toward science. Scientific advances have been perceived as threats to faith. Scientific pioneers have been imprisoned, executed or excommunicated for thought crimes against God.

Violence against scientists has abated within Christianity in recent centuries, but only because of the Church's loss of political and military power. To some extent the Roman Catholic Church has repented of its sin against science and scientists. In 1992 Pope John Paul II pardoned Galileo for proposing that the earth revolves around the sun. Only 350 years late!

The Vatican today boasts a Pontifical Academy of Sciences, established in 1936. As the Roman Catholic Church has accommodated to science to a certain extent, the religious crusade against science has shifted to the Evangelical and Fundamentalist branches of Christianity. And so the Christian animosity toward science continues.

I have something shocking to say. It may not be controversial to you now, but it was heresy to Christians not so long ago. The earth is round! That's right! It is a sphere. That statement might not be provocative to you, but it is to the Flat Earth Society. Members of the Flat Earth Society believe the Earth is flat. They consider any evidence to the contrary, such as photos of the Earth taken from space, to be fabrications of a "round Earth conspiracy" orchestrated by NASA and other government agencies.

They envision the Earth as a flat disc with the Arctic Circle in the center. Antarctica is not a continent at the South Pole, as the round earthers say. It is actually a 150-foot-tall wall of ice encircling the outer rim of the earth. They claim that NASA employees guard this ice wall to prevent people from climbing over it and falling off the edge of the world.

Although some flat earthers are joking, like the pastafarians (devotees of the Flying Spaghetti Monster), most of them are dead serious. There was an article in the *New Yorker* recently (May 30, 2018) describing the resurgence of this movement in the United States. They held a Flat Earth Conference in Raleigh, North Carolina, in November 2017.

To put this in perspective, it is important to remember that the Flat Earth theory was once accepted by every human being. That was before the philosopher Pythagoras theorized a round earth in the sixth century BC. The Old Testament assumes a flat earth. It speaks of "the four corners of the earth." (Isaiah 11:12) and "the ends of the earth." (Zechariah 9:10) Spheres do not have corners or ends! We take those expressions metaphorically, but in ancient times people took them literally.

Ancient Hebrew cosmology has a three tiered universe with earth at the center. It sees the earth as a flat surface resting on pillars. According to the Book of Job, earthquakes occur when these pillars shake. (Job 9:6) Above us is the firmament, which is a hard dome that covers the earth. Above the firmament is water, and sometimes the windows of heaven open and water falls. Below the earth is also water.

In the story of Noah's flood the windows of heaven and the floodgates under the earth opened for forty days and flooded the whole earth. Above the waters of heaven is the high heaven where God dwells. Below the subterranean waters is the underworld, called Sheol in the Old Testament. This is how the ancient Hebrews pictured the universe. It would have been heresy in biblical times to suggest the earth was round. But now I can say the earth is a sphere, and everyone reading my words agrees with me ... I hope.

I will say a second radical thing. The earth moves around the sun. The sun does not go around the earth, even though it appears that way when we trace the movement of the sun across the sky. But in fact the sun is the center of the solar system and not the earth. That was also a radical thing to say a few hundred years ago. Copernicus came up with the theory in 1543. Galileo was excommunicated from the Roman Catholic Church in 1633 for insisting on this heliocentric model.

The church believed that the sun moves around the earth because the Bible says so. The Church pointed to Psalm 104:5 which says, "He set the earth on its foundations; it can never be moved." If the Bible says the earth can't be moved, that settles it; it can't move around the sun. Psalm 19 says of the sun, "It rises at one end of the heavens and runs its circuit to the other." It says nothing about the earth rotating, giving the appearance of the sun moving across the sky.

The church also pointed to the Bible story of Joshua commanding the sun and the moon to stand still for 24 hours so he would have more daylight to kill Amorites. Can you imagine what that would mean if that literally happened? If the sun literally remained in the same position in the sky for 24 hours?

Not long ago it was obvious to everyone that the sun moved around the earth. It made perfect sense. It was conventional wisdom. Just look at the movement of the sun across the sky. We still talk about the sun rising and setting. But the church – and the Bible – were wrong. Today I could preach from the pulpit of even the most fundamentalist in America, proclaiming that the earth is round and revolves around the sun, and the congregation would agree. "Of course!" they would say, "What else is new?"

EVOLUTION

Now I will say another radical thing. All life on earth evolved from single-celled organisms over the last 3.8 billion years. Unlike my first two statements, that is still a controversial thing for a Christian pastor to say in the 21st century. I would not be welcomed to preach that message in most evangelical pulpits. It might be another 350 years before all Christians admit it is true.

But there is no doubt about the truth of evolution. There is no more doubt about evolution than there is about the earth being a sphere or that the earth orbits the sun. But your pastor may not tell you about evolution. He might not even believe it! There are a lot of Christians and churches who disagree with the theory of evolution. They think it is a secular humanist conspiracy to undermine the Bible.

Many Christians believe in Creationism. They believe that God made human beings and all other creatures in their present forms in six 24-hour days less than 10,000 years ago. According to the most recent Gallup survey taken in 2017, 38% of US adults believe in "young earth" creationism. That is 93 million people. That means that a lot of churches and pastors hold to creationist views.

In northern Kentucky not far from Cincinnati, the Creation Museum opened in 2007. It proclaims the gospel of six-day creationism. It has exhibits showing ancient children playing with dinosaurs. They believe and teach that humans and dinosaurs coexisted. In July 2016 they added a second theme park called the Ark Encounter, which showcases a life-size Noah's Ark that you can tour for only $48. A combo Creation Museum and Ark Encounter ticket is $70.

They take the stories of the Book of Genesis as literal history. The chances are very good that some of you reading this book – if the surveys are correct, maybe even 38% of you - are creationists and are offended by my unequivocal statement saying that evolution is true. If that is true of you, I encourage you to hear me out before automatically dismissing what I have to say.

Creationists say, "But evolution is only a theory. It isn't proven. That is why it is called the *theory* of evolution." That is a misunderstanding of the scientific use of the word "theory." In scientific parlance to say something is a theory is not to say it is hypothetical. This is the definition of a scientific theory according to the American Association for the Advancement of Science:

> A scientific theory is a well-substantiated explanation of some aspect of the natural world, based on a body of facts that have been repeatedly confirmed through observation and experiment. Such fact-supported theories are not 'guesses' but reliable accounts of the real world. The theory of biological evolution is more than 'just a theory.' It is as factual an explanation of the universe as the atomic theory of matter or the germ theory of disease. Our understanding of gravity is still a work in progress. But the phenomenon of gravity, like evolution, is an accepted fact.[23]

Evolution is a fact. Christianity needs to acknowledge it and adapt to this new reality. Pastors need to proclaim evolution as the work of God. The great hymn "Once to Every Man and Nation" puts it well: "New occasions teach new duties. Time makes ancient good uncouth. They must upward still, and onward, who would keep abreast of Truth." Christianity has not always kept abreast of truth.

Ever since Charles Darwin proposed natural selection in his 1859 book *On the Origin of Species,* Christianity has had a hard time accepting evolution. In fact it took Darwin 20 years from the time he conceived the idea until he published it, because he was afraid of the reaction it would receive from the Church. It turned out that Darwin's fears were justified.

Although Darwin was not excommunicated like Galileo (in fact he was honored with burial in Westminster Abbey), he has been demonized by conservative Christians for the last 160 years. They say Darwinism undermines the Word of God and thereby destroys the foundations of Christianity.

Darwin did not destroy anything, but he did revolutionize our thinking about the natural world. We can speak of a Darwinian revolution just as we speak of the Copernican revolution. Evolution revolutionized the natural sciences, and it has the potential to revolutionize Christian theology.

Even though I will explore Christian theology more fully in a future chapter, it is beneficial here to explore how the fact of evolution revolutionizes theology. Such a dramatic change in one's understanding of the doctrine of creation will necessarily impact every aspect of Christian theology, but for brevity's sake I will mention only four.

First, evolution revolutionizes the doctrine of Scripture. Some Christians accuse me not believing the Bible because I accept that evolution is true. They say that the Bible is the inerrant, infallible Word of God, which must be literally true or it is not true at all. But the Bible never says it should be taken literally.

As I have already noted under the section about the Bible, this is what Scripture says about itself: "All scripture is given by inspiration of God, and is profitable for doctrine, for reproof, for correction, for instruction in righteousness." 2 Tim 3:16 KJV) It calls scripture profitable or useful, not infallible. There is a big difference.

The Bible never claims to be inerrant, especially when it comes to science. When Psalm 19 refers to the Law as perfect, it is not talking about scientifically or historically inerrant. The Hebrew word perfect does not mean that. If you read the rest of the verse it is clear it is talking about its ability to convert or revive the soul. Psalm 19 is saying the same thing as the verse from Second Timothy.

Furthermore Scripture is just one form of divine revelation. According to classic Christian theology there are two types of revelation. One is called special revelation. That is Scripture. The other is called natural revelation. God speaks through the natural world. Genesis says that God spoke the heavens and the earth into existence. The universe is literally – according to the Bible – the Word of God.

That means that God speaks through the natural world, including the fossil record. God speaks through DNA. God speaks through natural processes such as the decay rate of radioactive isotopes. That is how scientists can date material; it is called radiometric dating or radioactive dating. God speaks through nature, and scientists can read what God wrote into the fabric of the universe billions of years ago.

God speaks the language of science as well as Hebrew and Greek. God speaks through scientists today, like he spoke through prophets centuries ago. God does not lie or contradict himself. (Numbers 23:19) God says through scientific evidence that the world is 4.5 billion years old, and the universe is 13.8 billion years old - not 10,000 years old. We misread the Bible if we take it literally.

Christians need to embrace the scientific method as a God-given way of discerning how God has worked and is working in the world today. The anti-science stance of so much of fundamentalist and evangelical Christianity cannot stand the test of time and will only hurt the proclamation of the Christian gospel in the long run.

No wonder church attendance is plummeting in America! People are not going to come to church if they have to check their brains at the door. There is no conflict between science and religion. We should not read the Bible literally; we should read it literately. We do that by being scientifically literate.

A second doctrine revolutionized by evolution is our understanding of Humanity, which used to be called the Doctrine of Man. Evolution reveals that the story of humanity is far older than previously thought. Our bodies are literally made of elements formed billions of years ago within stars.

Theoretical physicist Lawrence M. Krauss says, "The amazing thing is that every atom in your body came from a star that exploded. And, the atoms in your left hand probably came from a different star than your right hand. It really is the most poetic thing I know about physics: You are all stardust."[24] As Carl Sagan said, "The cosmos is within us. We are made of star-stuff." Now that is a creation story!

It does not negate the Bible's creation story. From Genesis we learn that we were made in the image of God. As the psalm says, we were made a little lower than God (some translations say a little lower than the angels.) The Bible teaches us about the intrinsic worth and sacredness of human life, but it doesn't tell us how we were made. Science does that.

Science and Scripture coincide in many places. We are literally made of the dust of the earth, as the Bible says. That does not mean that God formed a clay golem from the soil of Eden and breathed life into it, like a literal reading of the Bible says. But it means that we have come from the earth.

DNA evidence tells us that we are related to every other living thing on earth. Since the human genome was first sequenced in 2003, we have learned just how related we are to other living beings. We share 96 percent of our DNA with chimpanzees, but we also share 60 percent of our DNA with chickens and the fruit fly. The consequences of this for the Christian theology and ethics is tremendous. It means we are cousins to every living thing on earth. What a theological foundation for protecting and preserving our environment!

Third, evolution revolutionizes our understanding of Death. If you read the Bible literally it says that death only came into the world when

Adam and Eve sinned in the Garden of Eden. If they had not eaten of that darn Tree of Knowledge then they – and we - would have lived forever. But that Bible story is not meant to be taken literally. When we read those stories, it should be obvious that we are in the realm of symbols.

Science tells us that death has been around as long as life. The fossil record tells us that. It is the physical record of death. Death was around long before there were humans. There is no evolution without death. Death is a natural part of life. It is not the punishment of an angry God toward two rebellious humans in a paradisal garden. We have to reinterpret those stories of Genesis based on what we know is true. Then it seems clear that Genesis is talking about spiritual death, not physical death.

Fourth, evolution revolutionizes the doctrine of Salvation. There is still salvation, and Christ is still the Savior. You still have the Cross and the Resurrection, but what we are saved from and saved for is transformed when we listen to the Word of God revealed through the natural world. We are not saved from physical death but from spiritual death. We are not saved from the consequences of Adam and Eve eating fruit from the wrong tree. We are saved from our own sin. Adam and Eve are us. The story of the Garden of Eden is our story, not the story of ancient ancestors.

There is a lot more I could say, but I hope you get the point. And I hope that those of you who believe the earth was created in six 24-hour days a few thousand years ago will see that there is another way of being Christian. We can still believe in the biblical and theological doctrine of Creation without believing in Creationism. Those are two different things.

I encourage you to read not only the Scripture, which is the Word of God penned by men, but also the Word of God written by God's own hand in the fossil record, in our DNA and in the stars. The real story of Creation is far older, more intricate, more fascinating and awesome. God is so much bigger than we have imagined. All we need to do is open our hearts and our minds to the grandeur of God revealed through his creation.

CLIMATE CHANGE

Climate change is another area in which conservative Christians feel threatened by scientific research. Why this is the case is mystifying to me. Unlike evolution there are no clear doctrines in the Bible that are undermined by believing that the earth's climate is changing rapidly due to human advancements in technology. In fact it would seem to agree with the concept of original sin and God's curse upon the ground due to human disobedience.

Climate change would be the perfect example for conservative Christians to use to illustrate the dangers of science! It shows what happens when scientific progress grows unchecked by man's God-given responsibility to be stewards of the earth.

Yet many Christians have taken exactly the opposite stance. They deny climate change, even though the scientific evidence is clearly against them. Theologically speaking this makes no sense. Their stance appears to be the result of an unholy alliance between conservative politics and conservative Christianity.

Climate change is real. It is happening. Shrinking ice caps and retreating glaciers ought to be evidence enough. There is no doubt about it. Scientists are nearly unanimous in the conclusion that it is caused by human activity. That is the position of the Academies of Science from 80 countries, as well as many scientific organizations that study climate science. 97% of active climate researchers endorse this consensus conclusion.[25] Yet many Christians don't believe it. Furthermore they don't even believe that scientists believe it!

The Pew Research Center has conducted several surveys on this topic in the past decade. A 2014 survey revealed that overall, 50% of adults say climate change is occurring mostly because of human activity, such as burning fossil fuels. The numbers generally go down depending on how religious, and particularly how conservatively religious, one is. 64% of religiously unaffiliated people believe in human caused climate change, 41% of white mainline Protestants, and 28% of white evangelicals. [26]

The really interesting thing about this study is what people believe about the scientific consensus on global warming. 47% of white evangelicals think that scientists do not agree with the reality of climate change, while 45% believe scientists are generally agreed. Almost the same percentage (52% to 43%) of White mainline Protestants agreed. This shows the disparity between what scientists know and what Christians think scientists know. No one, not even the religiously unaffiliated (60% to 30%) came anywhere close to the reality that 97% of scientists are convinced of the reality of climate change.

Ignorance of the scientific evidence and scientific consensus on climate change is a problem. This is the result of an anti-science bias in our culture. I am not a scientist. Personally I do not know enough about science to interpret the scientific data for myself. But I trust that climate change scientists know what they are doing. Apparently that is not the case with most people, especially religious people.

It is not just religious people who are skeptical of the claims of scientists. Even anti-religious folk can be anti-science. In his scientific blog, physicist Rob Knop tells the story of meeting a postmodern deconstructionist. He writes:

> In one of my first couple of years as a physics professor at Vanderbilt, fellow astronomer David Weintraub introduced me to another faculty member we ran into at lunch. He was from one of the humanities departments — I forget which. When David introduced me as somebody who worked on measuring the expansion rate of the Universe, this other fellow's immediate response was that the only reason we astronomers believed in the Big Bang theory was because of our Judeo-Christian cultural bias that there was a moment of beginning.

> I was quite taken aback. I tried to talk about the Cosmic Microwave Background, light element ratios, and so forth, but he waved them all off. I mentioned that his assertion wasn't even historically correct: earlier in the 20th century, the steady-state model (the Universe has always been as it is now) was if anything the dominant cosmological model. His response to hearing the postcard description of the Steady State

Universe: "I like that one better." Scientific evidence be damned....

It was really quite an eye opener. I had run into a living stereotype of the post-modernist deconstructionist, who believes that absolutely everything is a social construction. He had quickly judged the intellectual output of a field of study he was ignorant about based on his own bias and methodology.[27]

The Big Bang and Climate Change are real. Even if the intellectual elite don't think so, and even if your pastor does not tell you so. It would behoove the Christian Church to get on board and readjust their theology and ethics to this new reality.

Woo Woo

As this discussion of Climate Change shows, it is not only religious conservatives who are in denial about certain scientifically established facts. The liberal wing of American religion and the nonreligious can be just as opposed to scientific truth. Liberals can be just as susceptible to magical thinking and pseudo-science as fundamentalists. In the realm of spirituality, especially with the "spiritual but not religious" crowd, anything goes.

Here are I speaking about such things as the anti-vaccine movement, homeopathy, astrology, Reiki, the healing properties of crystals and biomagnetism, Tarot, past life regression, channeling, angelology, numerology, UFOs, and a host of other beliefs and practices. I group them all collectively under the heading of "Woo."

Woo or woo-woo is a term made popular by Michael Shermer, the Founding Publisher of *Skeptic* magazine and a monthly columnist for *Scientific American*. He first used the term to refer to the beliefs of New Age star Deepak Chopra. It is now used to describe all sorts of pseudo-science, which is often linked to New Age spirituality.

Skeptico defines it this way: "Woo is a word skeptics use as shorthand to describe pseudo-scientific and often anti-scientific ideas - ideas that are irrational and not based on evidence commensurate with the extraordinary nature of the claim. These are ideas that usually rely on magical thinking, are rarely tested to see if they are real, and are usually resistant to reason and contrary evidence."[28]

I do not have the space in this book or the inclination to debunk all these practices. If you believe in one or more of them, then you probably will not listen to me anyway. I found this out firsthand when I got into a discussion (which quickly turned into an argument) over homeopathy with the owner of a local Natural Foods store. My statement that the theory behind homeopathy had been disproven years ago by scientific experiments did not matter to her in the least. She "knew" it worked. I asked her how she knew. She said it was because people had been buying the products from her for 30 years, and people would not buy them if they didn't work!

I told her about a biography I had just finished reading entitled *An American Princess*, about heiress Allene Tew. She married the wealthy Tod Hostetter, whose fortune came from the sale of Hostetter's "Celebrated" Bitters. It was a patented medicine that earned the family tens of millions of dollars in the 1800's, when a million dollars was a lot of money. The concoction was used as a cure-all by Union soldiers during the Civil War. It was advertised to them as "a positive protective against the fatal maladies of the Southern swamps, and the poisonous tendency of the impure rivers and bayous."

It was advertised as curing dyspepsia (indigestion), slow constitutional decay, nervous prostration, mental gloom, agues, colics, dysenteric pains, bilious complaints, and "dread diarrhea." It was composed of 47% alcohol (94 proof) and served in saloons by the glass (thereby curing mental gloom.) Hostetter sweetened the nostrum with sugar and added aromatic oils (anise, coriander) and vegetable bitters (cinchona, gentian) to give it a medicinal taste. And it worked! Thousands of people gave glowing testimonials that Hostetter Bitters healed all these diseases and more. But it worked only because people believed it worked. The truth is that it was the proverbial "snake oil."

I told my local snake oil salesperson that homeopathic "medicine" worked only when people believed it worked, like faith healing. It was at best a placebo effect. My effort at a rational refutation of homeopathy only infuriated her. It became clear to me that homeopathy served as a religion for her – as well as a livelihood – and no evidence I presented would make any difference. It was like trying to talk a Jehovah's Witness out of the use of the name Jehovah or talking a Mormon out of the Book of Mormon (both of which I have also tried with similar results.)

What is true of homeopathy is also true of many other beliefs and practices associated with New Age spirituality. People in the most liberal churches, in their attempt to be nonjudgmental and inclusive of all types of religious beliefs, have warmly embraced a strange collection of occult beliefs and magical practices. These are often described in scientific terms with plenty of anecdotal evidence to prove they work.

But in the end it is all just woo. It is just another way that religious people discount science.

.

4

WHAT YOUR PASTOR WON'T TELL YOU ABOUT CHURCH HISTORY

Chances are your pastor has not told you very much about the history of Christianity. It is not because he is keeping it a secret. Most people are not interested in it. Therefore they are ignorant about it. If they think about the differences between various branches of Christianity at all, it is probably in relation to their own denomination.

For example the church I am presently attending is doing a series on Methodism. The pastor wants his congregation to be informed about the basics of their brand of Christianity. I did the same thing at the Baptist church I served in Pennsylvania. I preached a series of sermons on distinctive Baptist beliefs and practices. That is as far as most pastors and churches go in exploring Christian history.

From taking history classes in high school or college, Christians may know the big picture of Christianity as part of the development of Western civilization. They will be able to distinguish between the Catholic and Protestant branches of Christianity, and perhaps Eastern Orthodox. Beyond that their knowledge probably is limited to the churches in their neighborhood or the religions practiced by their family members. They know that Jehovah's Witnesses and Mormons come knocking on their door, but they probably could not tell you the difference between the two sects.

When it comes to the origins of Christianity most Christians have only an elementary understanding. Jesus started it. The twelve apostles continued it. The Roman Catholic Church was part of the process. Somehow we got to the place we are today with over 30,000 different Christian denominations.

People see all forms of Christianity as basically teaching the same thing. They are like different flavors of ice cream. Everyone has a preference, and the differences are not very important. Many times I have heard laypeople sum it up this way: "We all worship the same God."

People have no idea how bewilderingly diverse early Christianity really was. They did not all worship the same God. The history of Christianity easily could have turned out very differently than it did. If a different Christian group had prevailed at a crucial moment in history, we could be worshipping two gods (as Marcionite Christianity did) or 30 gods (as in Gnostic Christianity) and still call it Christianity.

The scriptures, teachings and practices that Christians have today were not finalized until the fourth and fifth centuries. Jesus Christ was not the first Christian any more than John the Baptist was the first Baptist.

The twelve apostles did not invent Christianity. In fact, the Christianity that the earliest church practiced was very different in every way – theologically and ritually – than the Christianity that exists today. A Pharisee from southern Turkey named Saul had more influence on the present form of Christianity than either Jesus or the twelve apostles. It is not an exaggeration to say that the apostle Paul (as he called himself) is responsible for Christianity as we know it.

Paul is the founder of the religion we now call Christianity. Then it grew and changed beyond his wildest dreams. But Paul's gospel was just one of many types of Christianity (Bart Ehrman calls them "lost Christianities") which were struggling for survival in the first and second centuries. Only one survived.

It was definitely the survival of the fittest! There is a parallel to the evolutionary development of different species of humans that competed for dominance on this planet. Of the fifteen types of human species discovered so far, only Homo sapiens remains. Of the many Christianities, only the one we call orthodox survived. All modern forms of Christianity are descended from that one.

We see evidence of a variety of sects in the writings of the apostle Paul, which are the earliest documents in the New Testament. He writes to a divided Corinthian church: "What I mean is that each one of you says, 'I follow Paul,' or 'I follow Apollos,' or 'I follow Cephas,' or 'I follow Christ.'" (I Corinthians 1:12) Each one of these factions – and many others in early Christianity - thought they were right, that their gospel was the true gospel taught by Jesus and the original apostles.

The truth is that Christianity was a very diverse movement from the very beginning.[29] Then it evolved and changed even more over the centuries. In the beginning - in Jesus' time – there was no religion called Christianity. Jesus was not a Christian, and he did not envision founding a new religion with clergy and creeds. For Jesus and his earliest followers there was no time for such things. Jesus was an apocalyptic preacher who believed that the world was coming to an end very soon - within the lifetimes of those who heard him preach. The earliest Christians believed him.

Jesus proclaimed, "For whoever is ashamed of me and of my words, of him will the Son of Man be ashamed when he comes in his glory and the glory of the Father and of the holy angels. But I tell you truly, there are some standing here who will not taste death until they see the kingdom of God." (Luke 9:26-27, cf. Matthew 16:27-28; Mark 8:38-9:1)

In another passage Jesus describes the coming of this kingdom in more detail.

Immediately after the tribulation of those days the sun will be darkened, and the moon will not give its light, and the stars will fall from heaven, and the powers of the heavens will be shaken. Then will appear in heaven the sign of the Son of Man, and then all the tribes of the earth will mourn, and they will see the Son of Man coming on the clouds of heaven with power and great glory. And he will send out his angels with a loud trumpet call, and they will gather his elect from the four winds, from one end of heaven to the other. From the fig tree learn its lesson: as soon as its branch becomes tender and puts out its leaves, you know that summer is near. So also, when you see all these things, you know that he is near, at the very gates. Truly, I say to you, this generation will not pass away until all these things take place. Heaven and earth will pass away, but my words will not pass away. (Matthew 24:29-35

Jesus clearly expected that the apocalyptic figure of the "Son of Man" (which he may have identified with himself – at least the later church did) would come soon and establish the Kingdom of God on earth. It would happen within the lifetimes of his disciples. Therefore there was no need to organize a church and write doctrinal statements.

But didn't Jesus talk about the church? Probably not. The only two passages in which Jesus uses the word "church" (ἐκκλησία, both in Matthew: 16:13-20 and 18:15-20) are widely believed by biblical scholars to have been inserted into the mouth of Jesus by the author of the Gospel of Matthew or a later editor. They presuppose church leadership and a system for handling disputes that existed only later.

Jesus did not start Christianity. Neither did he preach the key doctrines that later came to be identified with Christianity. Jesus preached the Kingdom of God. His message was simple: "Repent! The Kingdom of God is at hand!" Only later did the gospel *of* Jesus become the gospel *about* Jesus. The distinctive message of the apostle Paul - that salvation is through the grace of God through faith in Christ –

is absent from the teachings of Jesus. It is not to be found in the synoptic gospels.[30]

Salvation through faith in Christ as savior – and not by works - was conceived by the apostle Paul, a man who never met Jesus or heard him preach. Paul never read the gospels because they had not been written yet. He apparently never even heard any of the sayings of Jesus or stories about Jesus found in the gospels, since he never refers to them in any of his writings.

Paul's gospel of salvation by faith alone – and not by keeping the Jewish Law - was to become the hallmark of orthodox Christianity. But in Paul's day it was contested by the apostles James and Peter, who personally knew what Jesus preached. Sixty years after Jesus' death and resurrection, the idea of salvation by faith was enshrined in the Gospel of John in the ubiquitous John 3:16. "For God so loved the world, that he gave his only Son, that whoever believes in him should not perish but have eternal life."

But this was not the only understanding of the gospel circulating after Jesus' death and resurrection. For three hundred years there was no consensus on how one attains eternal life. The earliest form of the gospel appears to be the one articulated by Jesus and later his brother James, who took over the leadership of the Jerusalem Church after Jesus' death. It was based on the keeping of the Jewish Law, including circumcision.

EARLIEST CHRISTIANITY WAS A JEWISH SECT

Jesus was a Jew. All his disciples were Jews. He preached to Jews. Jesus encountered an occasional Gentile during this travels and ministered to them, but he made it clear they were not his mission. He said to the Canaanite woman, "I was sent only to the lost sheep of the house of Israel." (Matthew 15:24)

He instructed his twelve disciples to preach only to the twelve tribes of Israel. "These twelve Jesus sent out, instructing them, 'Go nowhere among the Gentiles and enter no town of the Samaritans, but go rather to the lost sheep of the house of Israel.'" (Matthew 10:5-6) There was no time to expand his target audience because he firmly believed that the Kingdom of God would come before they finished preaching to Israel. He said, "Truly, I say to you, you will not have gone through all the towns of Israel before the Son of Man comes." (Matthew 10:23)

Earliest Christianity was an apocalyptic movement within first century Judaism. Jesus' followers worshiped in the temple and synagogue, and practiced the radical "interim ethic"[31] of the

119

Sermon on the Mount, as they awaited the Kingdom of Heaven. Their only distinguishing characteristic was that they believed that Jesus was the Messiah. Christianity began as a Jewish sect, and the earliest Christians wanted to keep it that way.

This earliest group of believers in Jerusalem preserved the Jewish nature of the gospel. They saw themselves simply as Jews who followed Christ. But as the promised Kingdom failed to materialize, and Gentile Christianity gained numbers and took the name of "Christians" (Acts 11:19-26), the original Jewish believers came to be a minority within their own faith. By the second century they were on the fringe of the new religion and became known as Ebionites.

The Ebionites got their name, according to Origen of Alexandria (c. 212 AD), from the Hebrew term ebyon, which means "poor." Jesus had said of himself, "Foxes have holes, and birds of the air have nests, but the Son of Man has nowhere to lay his head." (Matthew 8:20) Jesus said to his disciples, "Blessed are you who are poor, for yours is the kingdom of God." (Luke 6:20) They took Jesus seriously when he said, "Any one of you who does not renounce all that he has cannot be my disciple." (Luke 14:33).

They saw themselves following the instruction of Jesus to his original disciples. According to Matthew's gospel, "These twelve Jesus sent out, instructing them, 'Go nowhere among the Gentiles and enter no town of the Samaritans, but go rather to the lost sheep of the house of Israel. And proclaim as you go, saying, "The kingdom of heaven is at hand." Heal the sick, raise the dead, cleanse lepers, cast out demons. You received without paying; give without pay. Acquire no gold or silver or copper for your belts, no bag for your journey, or two tunics or sandals or a staff, for the laborer deserves his food.'" (Matthew 10:5-10)

Jesus led a movement of religious mendicants. He called his disciples to leave their homes, families and possessions and follow him around the Galilean and Judean countryside. They intentionally adopted a peripatetic lifestyle of poverty for the purpose of preaching and healing. Their ministry, like later monastic movements, was directed especially to the poor, outcasts, and sick. After Jesus' death and resurrection, the earliest Jewish followers of Jesus saw no reason to alter their Lord's practice or instructions.

Jesus said to the rich young ruler, "If you would be perfect, go, sell what you possess and give to the poor, and you will have treasure in heaven; and come, follow me." (Matthew 19:21) That was no different than what Jesus asked his others followers to do. It just so happened that this man had "great wealth." Christians today weave ingenious interpretations of this story to rationalize NOT taking Jesus literally, but the Ebionites did not engage in such sophistry. For them to follow Jesus meant to be poor, not unlike the Franciscans of a later century.

According to the Book of Acts voluntary poverty was the norm immediately after the Day of Pentecost. "And all who believed were together and had all things in common. And they were selling their possessions and belongings and distributing the proceeds to all, as any had need. And day by day, attending the temple together and breaking bread in their homes, they received their food with glad and generous hearts, praising God and having favor with all the people." (Acts 2:44-47) Earliest Christianity was a form of Jewish religious communism in which believers shared their possessions and continued to participate in the life of the Jewish Temple.

The fact that the believers in Jerusalem were poor is evidenced by the offering that Paul collected among the Gentile churches for the Jewish Christians in Jerusalem. In his letter to Rome Paul writes: "At present, however, I am going to Jerusalem bringing aid to the saints. For Macedonia and Achaia have been pleased to make some contribution for the poor among the saints at Jerusalem." (Romans 15:25-26)

The earliest Jewish followers of Jesus sought to continue in the simple lifestyle of Jesus. If it were not for the apostle Paul, Christianity would have remained a Jewish sect. The earliest Jewish Christians believed that Jesus was the Jewish Messiah sent from the Jewish God to the Jewish people in fulfillment of the Jewish Scriptures. They believed that to belong to the people of God, one needed to be Jewish. They observed the Sabbath, kept kosher, and circumcised all males.[32]

The most outspoken and evangelistic of this earliest Jewish form of Christianity appears to be the group that Paul addresses in his letter to the Galatians. Paul did not mind if Jewish believers observed their Jewish gospel among Jews in Jerusalem, but when they attempted to export it to the Gentiles in his churches, Paul responded vehemently. Paul calls them "the circumcision party" (Galatians 2:12) and condemns them in the strongest terms.

He writes, "But even if we or an angel from heaven should preach to you a gospel contrary to the one we preached to you, let him be accursed." (1:8) He says they are preaching "a different gospel" (1:6) and "distort the gospel of Christ." (1:7) He meant that they were preaching a gospel different than *his* gospel, which indeed they were. They would have replied that they were preaching the original gospel of Jesus.

Christian commentators today usually call them Judaizers and portray them as early heretics. They say that their gospel was an aberrant form of Christianity, which strayed from the true gospel, which was championed by Paul. In fact it seems to be the other way around. These Jewish believers were the original Christians, and Paul's gospel was the innovation and "heresy."

In Galatians Paul describes a visit by Peter to Antioch where Peter ate with Gentile believers, as Paul's gospel advocated. Then "certain men from James" came and reminded Peter that this was not acceptable behavior for Christians. It appears that James and the Jerusalem church (which presumably included the original twelve apostles) shared the views of these Judaizers or early Ebionites. Jewish Christians eating with Gentiles was a violation of Jewish Law, which needed to be observed by Christians according to the James.

On this occasion both Peter and Barabbas sided with James and the circumcision party against Paul. So it seems that Paul's form of inclusive Christianity, which did away with the Law, was a minority view both in Galatia and Antioch, as well as Jerusalem.

Of course that is not the way the Book of Acts pictures it. Acts portrays Paul's version of the gospel as being endorsed by the Jerusalem church. That is because Acts was written from a Pauline perspective. The traditional author of Acts is Luke, a Gentile Christian and traveling companion of Paul. How else would he portray it?

Scripture, like history, is written by the victors. The writings that made it into the New Testament were those that endorsed the theology of the winners, and they rewrote history accordingly. Acts 15 pictures the apostles in Jerusalem to be of one mind in endorsing Paul's gospel. The opponents are described as "the sect of the Pharisees," Jesus' archrivals in the gospels. Barnabas stands with Paul. Even Peter and James make speeches promoting the inclusion of Gentiles into the church without having to keep the Law. The text of a letter from the apostles to the "Gentile believers in Antioch, Syria and Cilicia" is included in the chapter. It speaks in glowing terms of "our beloved Barnabas and Paul" and disowns the men who were preaching the need to obey the Jewish Law.

According to the Book of Acts the matter was resolved then and there, and the church lived happily ever after, following in the footsteps of the apostle Paul. Not so fast! If that were the case, then the Ebionites would not have been so prominent in the second century, and the early Church Fathers would not have seen them as a threat. It seems that the earliest form of Jewish Christianity did not roll over and die.

But Jewish Christianity struggled, especially when Jerusalem and the temple were destroyed in 70 AD, and the original apostles died off. The Roman response to the Bar Kokhba revolt of 132–136 AD decimated the Jewish communities of Jerusalem and Judea. This effectively ended any influence that Jewish Christians had on the theological development of Christianity.

But there are reports of Ebionites surviving into the 11th and 12th centuries.[33] There are even Christian groups today who retain some of the Jewish beliefs and practices of the Ebionites. I know this firsthand because my brother-in-law belongs to such a group in Orlando, Florida.[34]

One wonders how the Ebionites would have told the story of Christianity if their position had prevailed. If the Ebionites had been the victors in the theology wars, what books would have made it into the New Testament? Perhaps the *Letter of Peter to James*, the brother of Jesus and head of the church in Jerusalem, would have been included in our Bible. In this pseudonymous letter Peter speaks of his "enemy" (Paul) who teaches Gentiles not to obey the Law and distorts his teaching. He says:

For some from among the Gentiles have rejected my lawful preaching and have preferred a lawless and absurd doctrine of the man who is my enemy. And indeed some have attempted, while I am still alive, to distort my words by interpretations of many sorts, as if I taught the dissolution of the Law. . . . But that may God forbid! For to do such a thing means to act contrary to the Law of God which was made to Moses and was confirmed by our Lord in its everlasting continuance. For he said, "The heaven and the earth will pass away, but not one jot or one tittle shall pass away from the Law. (Letter of Peter to James, 2:3–5)

Another work written (pseudonymously) by Clement, the first century bishop of Rome and disciple of Peter, quotes a letter from Peter to Paul. Peter is questioning Paul's credentials as an apostle, saying that Paul's brief vision of the risen Christ on the Damascus Road pales in comparison to the real apostles' long relationship with Jesus:

And if our Jesus appeared to you also and became known in a vision and met you as angry with an enemy, yet he has spoken only through visions and dreams or through external revelations. But can anyone be made competent to teach through a vision? And if your opinion is that that is possible, why then did our teacher spend a whole year with us who were awake? How can we believe you even if he has appeared to you? . . . But if you were visited by him for the space of an hour and were instructed by him and thereby have become an apostle, then proclaim his words, expound what he has taught, be a friend to his apostles and do not contend with me, who am his confidant; for you have in hostility withstood me, who am a firm rock, the foundation stone of the Church. (Homilies 17.19) [35]

If these letters (known as the Pseudo-Clementine writings) had made it into our Bible instead of the letters of Paul, Christianity would be very different today. If the *Gospel of the Ebionites* (a Hebrew version of Matthew's gospel missing the first two chapters) had made it into the New Testament instead of our present Gospel of Matthew, then our view of Jesus would be different. Paul would have been condemned as the false teacher, as a "Gentilizer," who was opposed by faithful Jewish-Christians like Peter, James, and the rest of the apostles. But that was not to be. It was Paul's vision of Christianity that triumphed.

Paul's gospel won because Paul was a very effective missionary, and the Gentile churches he founded grew and generally remained faithful to his gospel. Gentiles did not feel the need to convert to Judaism in order to follow Jesus. How many Gentile men would willingly go through the painful Jewish rite of circumcision and keep the Jewish Law when they had a Gentile form of Christianity readily available? It is no wonder that Gentile Christianity prevailed! As soon as Gentiles began entering the Pauline churches in great numbers, it was only a matter of time until Gentiles outnumbered Jews. The victory of Gentile Christianity and Paul's understanding of salvation was inevitable.

Ebionite Christianity understood the gospel of Jesus to be a continuation of Judaism, but with the important addition that Jesus was the Jewish Messiah. For Ebionite Christians, the Law given by God to Israel was eternally binding. Keeping "every jot and tittle" as Jesus put it, was necessary for salvation. In other words one had to become a Jew in order to be a follower of Christ.

Ebionite theology was very different from the Gentile theology that came to dominate Christianity. They understood Jesus to be fully human and not divine. Consequently they did not believe in Jesus' preexistence (as the Gospel of John teaches) or his virgin birth (as Matthew teaches).

For Ebionites Jesus was the Son of God, not because of his inherently divine nature or supernatural virgin birth, but because of his obedience and righteousness. He kept God's law perfectly and was the most righteous man on earth.

Therefore God adopted Jesus as his son at his baptism. As Hebrews 1:5 (and an early variant of Luke 3:22) says, "You are my Son; today I have begotten you." This kind of Christology is called "adoptionism."

According to Ebionism God chose Jesus to be his son and to sacrifice himself for the sake of others. As Jesus said, "The Son of Man came not to be served but to serve, and to give his life as a ransom for many" (Matthew 20:28). Jesus died on the cross as a punishment for the sins of the world. He was the perfect sacrifice, fulfilling God's promise of salvation for his chosen people, the Jews. Jesus' resurrection was a sign that God had accepted Jesus' sacrifice. They would have even agreed with Paul when he wrote that Jesus, "was descended from David according to the flesh and was declared to be the Son of God in power according to the Spirit of holiness by his resurrection from the dead, Jesus Christ our Lord." (Romans 1:3-4)

EARLY CHRISTIANITY WAS ANTI-SEMITIC

It is likely that your pastor has never told you about anti-Semitism in the New Testament and early Christianity. Anti-Semitism is taboo in the church these days. It is labeled "hate speech" and brings to mind memories of Nazism and the Holocaust. But the ugly truth is that there is a lot of "hate speech" the New Testament.

One of the early forms of Christianity was vehemently anti-Jewish. [36] This type of Christianity was so prevalent in the second and third centuries that the theologian Tertullian (155 – 240 AD) felt it necessary to write five volumes refuting it. It was called Marcionism, and was begun by a late first century – early second century Christian preacher (and son of a preacher) named Marcion.

But before we get to Marcion, we have to understand where he got his ideas. He did not invent anti-Semitism. Like so many people after him, he got them from the New Testament. In Matthew's Gospel, which is considered the most Jewish of the gospels, the Roman governor Pilate sees no reason to execute Jesus but the Jews insist. He tries to get Jesus released by offering to release a prisoner, but they choose Barabbas instead. Pilate declares he is innocent of Jesus' blood and (literally) washes his hands of the matter. The people respond, "His blood be on us and on our children!" (Matthew 27:25) This began the idea of the "blood curse" and the charge of deicide against the Jews.

In the Gospel of John, the last of the gospels to be written, anti-Jewish prejudice is pervasive. According to my former Greek professor, R. Alan Culpepper, the word Ἰουδαῖοι, (Ioudaioi), translated "the Jews," is used 63 times in the Gospel of John. 31 of those times it is used in a hostile manner.[37] In the Synoptic gospels (Matthew, Mark, and Luke) the Jewish enemies of Jesus are identified as certain groups of Jews: the chief priests, scribes and the elders. (Mark 11-17-28, Luke 20:1-2; Matthew 21:23.) But in John it is "the Jews" as a whole who are the enemies of Jesus.

In John "the Jews" are looking for a chance to kill Jesus (7:1-9). No one would speak openly for Jesus "fear of the Jews" (7:12-13). After Jesus' execution, the disciples hide behind locked doors, "for fear of the Jews." (20:19) John's gospel associates "the Jews" with darkness and with the devil. In John 8 Jesus says the Jews are children of the devil:

> I know that you are offspring of Abraham; yet you seek to kill me because my word finds no place in you. I speak of what I have seen with my Father, and you do what you have heard from your father .... You are of your father the devil, and your will is to do your father's desires. He was a murderer from the beginning, and does not stand in the truth, because there is no truth in him. When he lies, he speaks out of his own character, for he is a liar and the father of lies....Whoever is of God hears the words of God. The reason why you do not hear them is that you are not of God." (John 8:37-38, 44, 47)

In John's Gospel "the Jews" collectively are instruments of Satan and responsible for the death of Jesus and the persecution of the church. Later generations of Christians would read these words in the New Testament as justification for anti-Semitic pogroms. After all, the Jews brought it on themselves for killing God!

In the Book of Acts the Jews are the enemy of the nascent church, continually hounding the apostle Paul and following him from city to city. In Antioch Paul preached in the synagogue "But when the Jews saw the crowds, they were filled with jealousy and began to contradict what was spoken by Paul, reviling him." And then later: "But the Jews incited the devout women of high standing and the leading men of the city, stirred up persecution against Paul and Barnabas, and drove them out of their district." (Acts 15:45, 50)

Paul went to Iconium. "Now at Iconium they entered together into the Jewish synagogue and spoke in such a way that a great number of both Jews and Greeks believed. But the unbelieving Jews stirred up the Gentiles and poisoned their minds against the brothers." (Acts 14:1-2) They went on to Lystra. "But Jews came from Antioch and Iconium, and having persuaded the crowds, they stoned Paul and dragged him out of the city, supposing that he was dead." (14:19)

Paul describes his experience in his own words in his letter to the Thessalonians: "For you, brothers, became imitators of the churches of God in Christ Jesus that are in Judea. For you suffered the same things from your own countrymen as they did from the Jews, who killed both the Lord Jesus and the prophets, and drove us out, and displease God and oppose all mankind by hindering us from speaking to the Gentiles that they might be saved — so as always to fill up the measure of their sins. But wrath has come upon them at last!" (I Thessalonians 2:14-16)

I could give more examples, but you get the picture. In the New Testament the Jews are the enemies. No other racial or ethnic group are singled out for vilification the way the Jews are. In the synoptic gospels Jesus confines his criticism to certain groups of Jews, especially the Pharisees and Sadducees. But even there it is the Jewish leaders and people, not the Roman governor, who are responsible for the execution of Jesus.

At about the time the gospels were being written, a boy was born to a Christian bishop and his wife in Pontus, a region on the southern coast of the Black Sea, located in modern-day Turkey. The church in Pontus was one of the very first churches. Aquila and Priscilla, traveling companions of the Apostle Paul, were from Pontus. Marcion was raised as a Christian and was familiar with the Hebrew Scriptures as well as the letters of Paul.

The movement that bears his name was the exact opposite of the Ebionites. Whereas the Ebionites embraced all things Jewish, Marcion opposed all things Jewish. He embraced the anti-Semitism found in the New Testament and made it into a religion. His form of Christianity outdid Paul in opposing Judaizers and Jewish Christianity. For Marcion the Christian gospel demanded a complete break from the Jewish religion. That included a rejection of the Hebrew Scriptures and the Hebrew God.

From his study of the Hebrew Scriptures and the writings of the apostle Paul, Marcion concluded that the Jewish and Christian understandings of God were incompatible. The Law of the Jews and the Gospel of Christ were two entirely different ways of approaching the spiritual life. The Law had to do with commandments, judgment, punishment and death. The gospel was about grace, love, faith, forgiveness and eternal life. As the Gospel of John would say, "The Law was given through Moses; grace and truth came through Jesus Christ." (John 1:17)

Marcion was infatuated with the gospel proclaimed by the apostle Paul, which was presumably the gospel he had heard from his father. It taught that a person was justified by faith in Christ, not by the works of the Law. This was the foundation of Marcion's gospel. In fact he elevated the writings of Paul above all Scripture. Marcion is recognized by historians as the first Christian to define a canon of Christian scripture. It consisted of ten of the letters of Paul and an edited version of the Gospel of Luke, presumably because it was written by a Gentile and is the least Jewish of the gospels.

As Marcion read the Scriptures, he saw the God of the Jews as a jealous, vengeful, wrathful God. The God of Jesus was one of love, mercy and grace. He could not reconcile these two pictures of God, so he concluded that there were two Gods. The God of the Old Testament was the God of this world. He created this world. The God of Jesus was entirely different from this Jewish God. He had nothing to do with this world until he sent Jesus. The Old Testament God gave Law to a chosen people, the Jews. The Christian God did not have a chosen people. He was the God of all peoples.

The Christian God came into the world in the person of Jesus to save people from the God of the Jews. The Jewish God commanded his people to kill their enemies. Jesus commanded us to love our enemies. The Jewish God condemned. The Christian God saved. The Jewish God punished people with death for breaking the Law. The Christian God provided a way of a redemption through the death of Jesus, who paid the penalty for our sin.

According to Marcion this is the true Christian gospel. Many people miss this truth because they are blinded by the Jewish God of the material world. The original twelve apostles misunderstood Jesus because they were Jewish and continued to revere the Jewish Scriptures. That is why the risen Christ had to return to earth one last time and appear to Paul, who finally got it right.

As 2 Corinthians says: "In their case the god of this world has blinded the minds of the unbelievers, to keep them from seeing the light of the gospel of the glory of Christ, who is the image of God. For what we proclaim is not ourselves, but Jesus Christ as Lord, with ourselves as your servants for Jesus' sake." (2 Corinthians 4:4-5)

You can imagine how appealing this gospel was to people in that day. In fact, it is appealing to people today! It is common for Christians today to echo Marcion's words. Many modern Christians see the Old Testament God as very different from the New Testament God. Modern Christians struggle with the Old Testament and its violence, wrath, and judgment. They prefer the kinder, gentler God of Jesus. It is a very small step to see them as two different Gods.

Marcion's understanding of God influenced his understanding of Jesus. If the Christian God is not of this world, then neither was his Son. For Marcion Jesus could not possibly be part of this material world created by the hateful Jewish God. Therefore Christ must not have had a physical body. He was not born. He was a spirit who only appeared to be a human being. Marcion quoted Paul, saying, Jesus came "in the likeness of sinful flesh." (Romans 8:3). He did not actually have human flesh; it was only the *likeness* of flesh. The theological word for this position is Docetism.

Marcion was very successful in spreading his gospel in Asia Minor. According to Bart Ehrman,

> Marcion experienced an almost unparalleled success on the mission field, establishing churches wherever he went, so that within a few years, one of his proto-orthodox opponents, the apologist and theologian in Rome, Justin, could say that he was teaching his heretical views to "many people of every nation" (Apology 1.26). For centuries Marcionite churches would thrive; in some parts of Asia Minor they were the original form of Christianity and continued for many years to comprise the greatest number of persons claiming to be Christian. As late as the fifth century we read of orthodox bishops warning members of their congregations to be wary when traveling, lest they

enter a strange town, attend the local church on Sunday morning, and find to their dismay that they are worshiping in the midst of Marcionite heretics.[38]

Marcion's views were eventually rejected as heresy. But they were a dominant voice in the theological discussion of Christianity for centuries. The anti-Jewish sentiment found in the New Testament and the writings of Marcion continue to haunt Christianity up until the current day, producing periodic tides of anti-Semitism.

EARLY CHRISTIANITY WAS MYSTICAL

There was another major form of early Christianity, broadly known as Gnosticism. It was a very diverse movement, similar to the "spiritual but not religious" phenomenon of today. It was composed of people who valued spiritual experience, but were not enthusiastic about the institutional church or organized religion. Maybe that is why your pastor has not told you about it. He would prefer to keep you coming to church, rather than going it alone, like so many "spiritual but not religious" people do these days.

Gnosticism emphasized an individualized spiritual awareness of God and God's Kingdom. The orthodox form of Christianity, which came to

WHAT YOUR PASTOR WON'T TELL YOU

dominate the church, was more concerned about order and uniformity. It was characterized by clear lines of ecclesiastical authority and policing heresies. Gnosticism was concerned with the individual's experience of God and relationship with Christ.

The term Gnosticism comes from the Greek word gnosis, which means knowledge. Gnostics "know" the truth about spiritual reality. This was not theological knowledge involving correct doctrine, as orthodox Christianity came to understand truth. Gnostic knowledge was experiential. It was a personal spiritual experience of God. The Gnostics believed that spiritual experience was the essence of Christ's gospel. It was what Jesus meant by the Kingdom of God.

For the Gnostics Christianity was not about theological or ecclesiastical matters. It was about the mystical dimension of the spiritual life. They pointed to the Bible for confirmation of their perspective. There are mystical experiences throughout the Bible. The prophet Ezekiel had fantastic visions that can only be called mystical. Isaiah's vision of God on his throne (Isaiah 6) was a mystical experience. Jacob's ladder to heaven and his wrestling match with God were mystical experiences, as was Moses' experience of the burning bush.

In the New Testament, one whole book – the Revelation of John – is a series of mystical visions that John had while on the island of Patmos. The gospels have mystical experiences. The baptism of Jesus was a mystical experience for Jesus; so was his 40 day temptation in the wilderness. We are told in the gospels that Jesus often went off by himself to pray, which indicates that his spiritual relationship with God was central to his life. When Jesus talked to Nicodemus about being "born of the Spirit," he was speaking about the importance of spiritual experience.

The transfiguration of Jesus on the mountaintop was a mystical experience for three of Jesus' closest disciples. In all three gospels the Transfiguration is closely associated with Peter's confession of faith in Jesus as the Christ, indicating that an individual's awareness of Jesus as the Christ is more than just a doctrinal statement. The resurrection of Christ was certainly a powerful spiritual experience for the apostles, regardless of how one views the physicality of his resurrection. Paul's encounter with the risen Christ on the Damascus Road was clearly a mystical and not a physical encounter with Jesus.

Paul speaks of his mystical experiences in his letters. It is commonly accepted that Paul is talking about himself in 2 Corinthians when he boasts of spiritual experiences. "I must go on boasting. Though there is nothing to be gained by it, I will go on to visions and revelations of the Lord. I know a man in Christ who fourteen years ago was caught up to the third heaven — whether in the body or out of the body I do not know, God knows. And I know that this man was caught up into paradise—whether in the body or out of the body I do not know, God knows — and he heard things that cannot be told, which man may not utter." (2 Corinthians 12:1-4)

Gnosticism draws on this stream of the biblical witness. It sees spiritual awareness and experience of Christ to be the heart of true religion and the Christian gospel. We see echoes of this today in the Pentecostal experience of "speaking in tongues" and other "supernatural" spiritual gifts. It is also evidenced in evangelical Christianity's emphasis on being "born again" and having a "personal relationship with Jesus Christ." The difference is that Evangelicalism combines the gnostic theme of spiritual experience with the orthodox emphasis on the necessity of correct doctrine for salvation.

The Gnostic understanding of the gospel is at least as old as orthodoxy. The oldest extant gnostic text is the Gospel of Thomas. It is a gospel composed entirely of sayings of Jesus. Such a gospel was theorized by scholars before it was found. For years Biblical scholars deduced the existence of a proto-gospel that was older than any gospel in our New Testament.

It was labeled Q, from the German word for source, Quelle. Q was an explanation for the fact that the Gospels of Matthew and Luke obviously copied many of the sayings of Jesus word-for-word from the same older source, which was not available to the writer of the Gospel of Mark. But no such ancient gospel of sayings had been found.

Then in 1945 a treasure trove of ancient manuscripts was found in the desert of Upper Egypt. They are now known as the Nag Hammadi library. They were Gnostic texts, and they opened up our understanding of early Christianity and Gnostic Christianity in particular. The oldest of the texts is the Gospel of Thomas, which is a gospel composed only of the sayings of Jesus – like the theorized Q source.

Thomas includes parallels to many of the sayings found in our canonical gospels. The composition of the Gospel of Thomas is dated to the same time as Matthew, Mark, and Luke. As such it tells us that Gnostic Christianity is as old as orthodox Christianity. It is possible that Gnosticism is even older, since there are documents in the Nag Hammadi library that appear to be pre-Christian.

It is difficult to summarize Gnostic Christianity beyond its mystical knowledge of God and Christ.

WHAT YOUR PASTOR WON'T TELL YOU

The Nag Hammadi codices reveal that there were many forms of Gnosticism. A modern parallel would be the "New Age" section of a modern bookstore. It would be difficult to find any two books on those shelves that agreed on any set of beliefs. Yet they are all grouped together as "New Age." It was the same with ancient Christian Gnosticism.

In Gnosticism, like in New Age, beliefs are of secondary importance. Yet we can identify some common themes that pop up regularly in Gnosticism. One is the unknowability of God. At first reading this would seem to contradict the name "gnostic" since Gnostics claimed to "know." Yet for the Gnostics, one can only know God with the heart, not the intellect. One cannot *know* anything *about* God, much less *say* anything about God. The Divine is by nature humanly incomprehensible.

For Gnostics God is the One. God is pure spirit, perfect and beyond description. God is incomparable to anything else in human experience and knowledge. To say anything about God would be to make a false statement. It is not unlike the Sanskrit expression "neti, neti" – "not this, not that." You can see why Gnostics would have a difficult time with orthodox Christians, as well as Ebionites and Marcionites. They made theological truth claims that Gnostics said were impossible to make without misrepresenting God.

Another general characteristic of Gnosticism is its view of the material world. Gnosticism was radically dualistic. It looked at the world and saw the reality of suffering and evil. It explained evil and suffering by saying that the material world is inherently evil, in contrast to the spiritual realm which is inherently good. This was in direct opposition to the Hebraic worldview, which viewed the material world as good.

The biblical book of Genesis says the world was created by a good God, who made all things and declared them "good." The Biblical authors, generally speaking, see suffering and evil as foreign intrusions into the world, caused either by human sin or an evil being called Satan. Gnosticism did not see it that way. For Gnostics the material world was not created by a good God and was not good.

For Gnostics, the easiest way to explain evil and suffering in the world was to say this was simply the way it is. It is the nature of the world. The world is bad and filled with suffering. But Gnostics could not just leave it at that. They came up with a host of myths to explain how this evil world emerged from the perfect One. These myths describe how various other entities emanated from the One. Gnostics called them aeons. The aeons in turn produced other entities. This realm of aeons was called the Fullness or Pleroma. It becomes very confusing very quickly.

The general idea is that there is a gradual downward trend from the perfect, pure, and good realm of Spirit to the evil and imperfect world of matter. The host of intermediary beings is thought to put enough distance between the original good God and the world to explain how we got into the mess we find ourselves. Somewhere along the way a lesser entity emerged who was imperfect and evil. That being is the Old Testament God, the creator of this imperfect and evil world in which we live.

Likewise human beings – at least our physical bodies – were created by this Old Testament God. Different Gnostic Christianities understood the nature of humans differently. For some sects all humans had a hidden essence of the original spirit world within them. For others only some humans had this spark of the divine. These elite humans, of course, were the Gnostics.

The goal of Christianity according to Gnosticism is to escape from this world and return to the heavenly realm. Humans – or at least the Gnostics – are not of this world. As the old hymn says, "This world is not my home, I'm just passing through." We are imprisoned in this material world and need to be saved. The way of salvation comes through gnosis (spiritual knowledge), and gnosis comes through Jesus Christ.

Jesus was viewed differently by different Gnostic groups. For some he was purely human, but he was a human who had realized his true spiritual nature and was able to pass that knowledge on to others. He was a Buddha type figure.

Some Gnostics made a distinction between Jesus and Christ. Christ is the spiritual entity who entered into Jesus at his baptism, and who taught humans how to be liberated from this material world. Christ then left Jesus while he was dying on the cross, prompting the human Jesus to cry out, "My God, my God, Why have you forsaken me." Some Gnostics say that the heavenly Christ returned to the human body of Jesus while he was in the tomb, thereby raising him from the dead.

But for some Gnostics their Savior could not possibly have been in a material body, which is necessarily evil. Jesus must have been a pure spiritual being who only appeared to be a human being. These Gnostics adopted the Docetic view of Christ. This was apparently the form of Gnosticism confronted by the author of the Second and Third Letters of John.

The author of these epistles says, "Many deceivers, who do not acknowledge Jesus Christ as coming in the flesh, have gone out into the world. Any such person is the deceiver and the antichrist." (2 John 1:7) And also, "This is how you can recognize the Spirit of God: Every spirit that acknowledges that Jesus Christ has come in the flesh is from God, but every spirit that does not acknowledge Jesus is not from God. This is the spirit of the antichrist, which you have heard is coming and even now is already in the world." (1 John 4:2-3) Clearly these Gnostics were not seen by the Johannine Christians as fellow Christians.

Gnosticism was known to the author of First Timothy. In that book it is even called by name. "O Timothy, guard what has been entrusted to you, avoiding worldly and empty chatter and the opposing arguments of what is falsely called knowledge" (I Timothy 6:20). The early Church Fathers Irenaeus and Tertullian thought that First Timothy 1:4 was referring to the elaborate Gnostic myths and genealogies of divine beings, when it says, "As I urged you when I was going to Macedonia, remain at Ephesus so that you may charge certain persons not to teach any different doctrine, nor to devote themselves to myths and endless genealogies, which promote speculations rather than the stewardship from God that is by faith." (I Timothy 1:3-4)

For Gnostics salvation was through spiritual knowledge. Not intellectual knowledge of correct Christian doctrine as with the orthodox. Not moral knowledge of the Law as with the Ebionites. It was, as Theodotus described it in the third century, "knowledge of who we were and what we have become, of where we were and where we have been made to fall, of where we are hastening and from where we are being redeemed, of what birth is and what rebirth."[39]

Salvation is through experiential awareness of our true nature. With that self-knowledge comes the experience of being who we truly are. It is a return to the Source of our existence in the One who is the true God. This knowledge was revealed by Jesus Christ when he walked the earth, and it is revealed by Jesus Christ today to those who ask, seek, and knock until the door to our true selves is opened. The Gnostics say that this is the gospel taught by Jesus.

This brief tour through three major movements within early Christianity shows us that the history of Christianity is not as simple as most Christians assume. Christians are taught (if taught at all) that the Christianity that exists today – as represented in the beliefs shared by Roman Catholic, Eastern Orthodox and Protestant Christianity - was the original Christianity of Jesus and the apostles. They are told that all other types of Christianity are later heresies, created by false teachers who knowingly and willfully corrupted the pristine message of the apostles.

But the truth is we don't know for sure what Jesus or the original apostles believed and preached. Jesus left no writings. Neither did any of the original twelve apostles. The New Testament books that bear the names of apostles – Matthew, Peter, John – are all pseudonymous works. All we know about Jesus and the Twelve is what ancient documents say Jesus and the apostles believed. These were written by later anonymous Christians after the original disciples had already died. These include, but are not limited to, the books in our New Testament.

From what we can discern using time-tested methods of historical research, Jesus appears to have been a Jewish apocalyptic preacher who proclaimed a coming Kingdom of Heaven. He believed that this coming Reign of God was to appear very soon, within the lifetimes of his hearers. It was to be accompanied by the fall of Jerusalem and ushered in by a heavenly figure known as the Son of Man.

The first apostles followed Jesus' beliefs, moral teachings and example, holding to an early form of Jewish Christianity later known as Ebionism. They identified Jesus as both the promised Jewish Messiah and the coming Son of Man. They kept the Law, worshipped in the Temple, and awaited the Kingdom of God. As the Kingdom tarried, and Christianity spread to the Gentile world through the ministry of

Paul of Tarsus, this earliest Christianity gave way to other forms of Christianity.

As far back as we can trace its history, using ancient canonical and non-canonical documents, Christianity was a family of faiths. In the first century there were many types of Christianities, of which our present-day form of Christianity – later called orthodox (meaning "right belief" or "right praise") was only one. All these various Christianities understood their gospel to be the original and most genuine form of Christianity.

This growing movement called Christianity became more varied in the second and third centuries, as each branch produced more branches. Christianity of the early centuries was more prolific and multifarious than today's Christianity, even when one defines Christianity broad enough to include sects like the Mormons, Jehovah's Witnesses, Christian Science, the Unification Church, and others.

It was not until three hundred years after Jesus that one form of Christianity – the orthodox – came to dominate the rest. It accomplished this feat by using the power of the Roman Empire, headed by the newly converted emperor Constantine. One type of Christianity became the official religion of Rome; all other types were banned. Heterodox scriptures and writings were burned or left to decompose through neglect. In spite of official opposition, some of these ancient forms of Christianity continued for centuries until they eventually went extinct and were forgotten. That is the untold history of the Christian church.

.

5

WHAT YOUR PASTOR WON'T TELL YOU ABOUT CHRISTIAN THEOLOGY

Christianity comes as a theological package. That is especially true if you are part of a conservative or evangelical church. Christians are expected to buy into the whole theological system. It is not "pick and choose;" it is "take it or leave it." It is not a spiritual buffet where you can select the doctrines you prefer and reject the ones you dislike. It is more like the old "blue plate special" at the local diner; there are no substitutions.

Christians can't choose reincarnation over resurrection or opt to worship Krishna over Yahweh. Christianity, for the most part is a package deal. If your pastor questions the essential beliefs of Christianity, she will find herself the target of self-appointed theological watchdogs, who are always on the lookout for heretics. Even in more liberal Christian denominations there is a limit to how far a pastor can bend doctrinal definitions without finding himself unemployed and unemployable.

But the truth is that many Christians do not accept all the teachings of Christianity, and that includes clergy. Your pastor might not accept all the traditional doctrines of orthodox Christianity – at least not literally. That is something your pastor is probably not advertising to the congregation or community. Another truth is that most Christians' understandings of doctrine differ significantly from the orthodox definitions.

According to Barna Research, 75% of American identify themselves as Christians, but only 56% believe Jesus was God. A majority, 52%, believe Jesus committed sins like other people,[40] contradicting several New Testament books.[41] A 2016 survey conducted by LifeWay Research found that large percentages of American Christians either reject or modify essential doctrines, such as the Trinity, Christ, salvation, and heaven. Many hold to theological views that mirror ancient heresies condemned by orthodox Christianity.

This led G. Shane Morris, senior writer at BreakPoint, a program of the Colson Center for Christian Worldview, to entitle his article about the

LifeWay survey: "Survey Finds Most American Christians Are Actually Heretics." He writes, "These are not minor points of doctrine, but core ideas that define Christianity itself."[42] Christians today are not a uniform – or an orthodox - bunch. We are as diverse today as Christians were in the early centuries of our religion, and just as heretical.

Even the theologians who hammered out Christian orthodoxy – the early Church Fathers – held some unusual ideas. Justin Martyr believed in annihilationism, that the souls of the evil cease to exist. He also had the interesting belief that Satan only sinned after Jesus came to earth. Tertullian believed that after baptism a Christian only had one additional opportunity for forgiveness. He also thought that demons invented jewelry for women to wear, and that is the real reason demons were condemned to hell. He called women "the gateway of the devil."

Origen believed in universalism (that everyone is saved), as did Gregory of Nazianzus and Gregory of Nyssa. The latter two were part of the First Council of Constantinople, which formulated the final form of the Nicene Creed, the gold standard of orthodox theology. Augustine believed that infants who were not baptized went straight to hell. He also believed in purgatory. Even the "orthodox" held some unorthodox beliefs.[43]

The historical reality is that Christianity did not come fully formed from the lips of Jesus or the apostles. Christian doctrine developed over centuries, and it was a very messy process. The earliest widely accepted doctrinal statement is known as the Apostles Creed, which is based on the older Roman Creed, also known as the Old Roman Symbol. The Apostles Creed is included in most hymnals and regularly recited by many congregations today. It reads:

I believe in God the Father Almighty,
Maker of heaven and earth:
And in Jesus Christ his only Son our Lord,
Who was conceived by the Holy Ghost,
Born of the Virgin Mary,
Suffered under Pontius Pilate,
Was crucified, dead, and buried:
He descended into hell;
The third day he rose again from the dead;
He ascended into heaven,
And sitteth on the right hand of God the Father Almighty;
From thence he shall come to judge the quick and the dead.
I believe in the Holy Ghost;
The holy Catholic Church;
The Communion of Saints;
The Forgiveness of sins;
The Resurrection of the body,

And the Life everlasting.
Amen.[44]

This creed is as important for what it does not say as for what it does say. It reflects a time before the Christological and Trinitarian controversies that prompted the careful wording of the fourth century Nicene Creed. It mentions all three "persons" of the Trinity, but does not explain how they are related or that all of them are equally divine. Arius, who was later condemned as a heretic, could have signed his name to this creed.

Indeed, both liberals and conservatives can recite this creed in good conscience, as long as they are not required to take the ideas literally. Figurative and allegorical interpretations go all the way back to scripture itself. Jesus – or at least the gospel writers – gave allegorical interpretations of his parables.

In his Letter to the Galatians Paul interprets the Old Testament figures of Sarah and Hagar allegorically. He writes: "Now this may be interpreted allegorically: these women are two covenants. One is from Mount Sinai, bearing children for slavery; she is Hagar. Now Hagar is Mount Sinai in Arabia; she corresponds to the present Jerusalem, for she is in slavery with her children. But the Jerusalem above is free, and she is our mother." (Galatians 4:24-26)

Origin taught that scripture – and Christian doctrine - had three levels of meaning. There is the physical level where scripture was interpreted literally. There is a second level that deals with personal relationships and experiences. The truest sense is symbolic and spiritual. By employing this method Christians can make scripture – and creeds based on scripture – mean anything they want.

Almost any Christian – liberal or conservative – can recite the words of the Apostles Creed today, because it does not define its terms. It does not define God except as Creator. It does not define what it means to call Jesus God's Son. It does not define the Holy Spirit. It does not describe how one is saved. It even leaves room for Jesus being resurrected spiritually instead of bodily.

Following the Apostle Paul's lead in I Corinthians, one can argue that the resurrection of believers refers to a "spiritual body," whatever that is! Gnostics could mouth the words of Apostles Creed in good conscience, while editing and interpreting it in their minds. That is the way many church members and pastors recite the Apostles Creed today. It would take the framers of the Nicene Creed in the fourth century to close the loopholes.

Today's Christianity owes its beliefs to the Nicene and Chalcedonian creeds of the fourth and fifth centuries. It was a long strange trip from the utterances of Jesus in the first century to the carefully worded doctrinal statements composed hundreds of years later. Jesus never would have recognized the Nicene Creed as his gospel. Neither would have his original disciples.

Read the words of the Nicene Creed. It is the only authoritative ecumenical statement of faith accepted by Roman Catholic, Eastern Orthodox, Oriental Orthodox, Anglican, and the major Protestant denominations. Therefore it is normative for today's Christianity.[45]

We believe in one God,
the Father, the Almighty,
maker of heaven and earth,
of all that is, seen and unseen.

We believe in one Lord, Jesus Christ,
the only Son of God,
eternally begotten of the Father,
God from God, Light from Light,
true God from true God,
begotten, not made,
of one substance with the Father.
Through him all things were made.
For us and for our salvation
he came down from heaven:
by the power of the Holy Spirit

he became incarnate from the Virgin Mary,
and was made man.
For our sake he was crucified under Pontius Pilate;
he suffered death and was buried.
On the third day he rose again
in accordance with the Scriptures;
he ascended into heaven
and is seated at the right hand of the Father.
He will come again in glory to judge the living and
the dead,
and his kingdom will have no end.

We believe in the Holy Spirit, the Lord, the giver of
life,
who proceeds from the Father and the Son.
With the Father and the Son he is worshiped and
glorified.
He has spoken through the Prophets.
We believe in one holy catholic and apostolic Church.
We acknowledge one baptism for the forgiveness of
sins.
We look for the resurrection of the dead,
and the life of the world to come. Amen.

Except for a few words and phrases here and
there, you will find nothing like this anywhere in the
New Testament, much less the Old Testament. Some
phrases are clearly foreign to the Biblical world.
Phrases like "God from God, Light from Light, true
God from true God, begotten, not made, of one

substance with the Father" would have puzzled the twelve apostles. Can you image Jesus, or even the apostle Paul, talking like this? This statement about the nature of Christ hails from Greek philosophy, not the Hebraic worldview of the Bible. Yet it is the orthodox understanding of Christology.

It is not my intention to explore the Nicene Creed or the controversies and heresies that prompted it. I simply want to identify it as the source of today's Christianity. It is assumed in most churches that Christian beliefs have remained the same since the beginning. It is thought that Christians today believe what the apostles believed. Ours is "the faith once for all delivered to the saints" (Jude 3). It is presumed that certain basic doctrines have been passed down faithfully from Jesus and his apostles for two thousand years. That is not true.

Orthodoxy is just the word used to describe the theology of the winners. (I am using the word "orthodoxy" to refer to traditional Christian doctrine, not the Eastern Orthodox branch of Christianity.) What passes as the gospel in all major branches of Christianity does not bear any resemblance to the original teaching of Jesus or the twelve apostles.

For the rest of this chapter I want to explore some of the doctrines held by Christians today and see if they have scriptural legitimacy. Because the nature of

Christ was foremost in the minds of the early Christians and the framers of the Nicene Creed, I will tackle that subject first.

JESUS WAS NOT WHO YOU THINK HE IS

Christians did not always believe that Jesus was God or even the Son of God. The earliest Jewish followers of Jesus almost certainly did not believe this. Today all branches of Christianity officially hold that Jesus was and is God. As the previously quoted Barna survey shows, a majority of Christians – but far from all – today agree.

The Nicene Creed (adopted in 325 at the First Council of Nicaea and amended at the First Council of Constantinople in 381) was formulated to make it clear that Jesus was fully God as well as fully human. It reads: "We believe in one Lord, Jesus Christ, the only Son of God, eternally begotten of the Father, God from God, Light from Light, true God from true God, begotten, not made, of one substance with the Father." It explains that this God "became incarnate from the Virgin Mary, and was made man." That has been the official stand of the Christian church ever since, even though few Christians could explain what those phrases mean.

The Chalcedonian Creed of 451 confirmed that Jesus was "truly God and truly Man" and explained how a man could be both, saying that Jesus had two natures, divine and human. "Acknowledged in two natures unconfusedly, unchangeably, indivisibly, inseparably; the difference of the natures being in no way removed because of the union, but rather the properties of each nature being preserved, and (both) concurring into one Person and one hypostasis."

This is not the way the earliest church thought of Jesus. In his book *How Jesus Became God*, New Testament scholar Bart Ehrman writes: "Jesus was not originally considered to be God in any sense at all, and ... he eventually became divine for his followers in some sense before he came to be thought of as equal with God Almighty in an absolute sense. But the point I stress is that this was, in fact, a development. One of the enduring findings of modern scholarship on the New Testament and early Christianity over the past two centuries is that the followers of Jesus, during his life, understood him to be human through and through, not God. "[46]

When we come to the final form of the New Testament, we find that most of the authors of the New Testament believed that Jesus was God. This is what one would expect, because any Christian writings that explicitly denied the deity of Christ were culled from the canon of sacred writings.

WHAT YOUR PASTOR WON'T TELL YOU

The Gospel of John begins by declaring that Jesus preexisted as the eternal Logos (Word, Reason, or Plan), a concept he borrowed from Greek philosophy. "In the beginning was the Word, and the Word was with God, and the Word was God.... And the Word became flesh and dwelt among us, and we have seen his glory, glory as of the only Son from the Father, full of grace and truth." (John 1:1, 14) This Gospel ends with "doubting" Thomas having a change of heart and declaring to Jesus, "My Lord and my God!" (John 20:28)

Other late New Testament writings follow suit in ascribing divinity to Jesus. The Letter to Titus refers to Jesus as "our great God and Savior Jesus Christ." (Titus 2:13) In like manner Second Peter calls him "our God and Savior Jesus Christ." 2 Peter 1:1)

The Apostle Paul, whose writings are the earliest documents in the New Testament, also believed Jesus was God. Quoting an early Christian hymn or creed, he writes, "Christ Jesus, who, being in very nature God, did not consider equality with God something to be used to his own advantage; rather, he made himself nothing by taking the very nature of a servant, being made in human likeness." (Philippians 2:5-7 NIV) In Romans 9:5 he refers to Jesus as "Christ, who is God over all."

But in the canonical gospels we can glimpse a time before Christians believed that Jesus was God. The Christological high point of the synoptic gospels is Peter's famous confession of faith, which addresses the question of Christ's identity. We know it best from Matthew's gospel.

> Now when Jesus came into the district of Caesarea Philippi, he asked his disciples, "Who do people say that the Son of Man is?" And they said, "Some say John the Baptist, others say Elijah, and others Jeremiah or one of the prophets." He said to them, "But who do you say that I am?" Simon Peter replied, "You are the Christ, the Son of the living God." And Jesus answered him, "Blessed are you, Simon Bar-Jonah! For flesh and blood has not revealed this to you, but my Father who is in heaven. And I tell you, you are Peter, and on this rock I will build my church, and the gates of hell shall not prevail against it. (Matthew 16:13-18)

Here Jesus is declared to be "the Christ, the Son of the living God." But the earliest gospel – the Gospel of Mark – records this scene differently, and it is confirmed by the Gospel of Luke. In Mark Peter declares simply "You are the Christ." (Mark 8:29) Luke expounds a little upon that simple statement saying, "You are the Christ of God." (Luke 9:20)

Christ is the Greek word for Messiah, which means "the anointed one." In Mark and Luke, Jesus is simply declared to be the Jewish Messiah, which in first century Jewish thinking was a purely human figure. There are no declarations of divinity in the earliest strata of the synoptic gospels.

Even the term "Son of God," as used by Matthew and elsewhere in the New Testament, does not necessarily mean that Jesus was considered divine in that same sense as the God of the Old Testament. Today we use the term "Son of God" and we assume it means that Jesus had the same nature as God. That is not the way it is used in the Old Testament, or even all times in the New Testament.

In Genesis 6:1-4 "sons of God" interbred with "daughters of man." It says, "The Nephilim (the KJV calls them "giants") were on the earth in those days, and also afterward, when the sons of God came in to the daughters of man and they bore children to them. These were the mighty men who were of old, the men of renown." The identity of these sons of God is a mystery, although interpretations range from fallen angels and polytheistic deities to human descendants of Seth.

In the Book of Job God lives with a group of heavenly beings called the sons of God, among whom is "the adversary" - Satan. (Job 1:6; 2:1) It appears that these "sons of God" are a heavenly council of divine beings, as found in other Ancient Near Eastern cosmologies. To preserve monotheism, later Christian interpretations would identify them as angels.

This multiplicity of gods is echoed in one of the two most common names for God in the Old Testament: Elohim, which is plural. For example in Genesis 1:26 Elohim says, "Let us make man in our image, after our likeness." Once again Christians get around this implied polytheism by saying that this is a "royal plural," like that used by Queen Elizabeth today. But it most likely points to a time in Israel's prehistory when there were many gods. This appears to be the meaning of the term "sons of God" in Job 38:6-7, which describes the moment of creation. "On what were its bases sunk, or who laid its cornerstone, when the morning stars sang together and all the sons of God shouted for joy?"

In other places the term "sons of God" refers to humans. "Remember the days of old; consider the years of many generations; ask your father, and he will show you, your elders, and they will tell you. When the Most High gave to the nations their inheritance, when he divided mankind, he fixed the borders of the peoples according to the number of the sons of God. But the Lord's portion is his people, Jacob his allotted heritage." (Deuteronomy 32:7-9)

Israel is referred to as God's son in Exodus 4:22 "Thus says the Lord, Israel is my firstborn son." It is used in the same way in Hosea and later quoted in the Gospel of Matthew as a prophecy of the holy family's flight to Egypt. "When Israel was a child, I loved him, and out of Egypt I called my son." (Hosea 11:1; Matthew 2:15)

A king is referred to as the Son of God, both in Israel and in pagan nations. Solomon and his descendants were considered sons of God. "I will be to him a father, and he shall be to me a son." (2 Samuel 7:14) Psalm 2 is a coronation psalm for the kings of Israel, in which God says, "You are my Son; today I have begotten you." (Psalm 2:7) This psalm is quoted in the New Testament as referring to Jesus as the Messiah. (Hebrews 5:5)

Jesus referred to human peacemakers as "sons of God." (Matthew 5:9) Elsewhere he refers to humans who are raised from the dead in the future Kingdom of God as "sons of God" and "like angels." (Luke 20:35-37) In several places the Apostle Paul refers to Christians as "sons of God." (Romans 8:14, 19; Galatians 3:26)

These examples are enough to make it clear that the term "Son of God" could have a range of meanings for the earliest Jewish Christians, without implying that Jesus shared godhood with his

Heavenly Father. The Jewish Encyclopedia remarks, "Yet the term by no means carries the idea of physical descent from, and essential unity with, God the Father. The Hebrew idiom conveys nothing further than a simple expression of godlikeness."[47]

It was undoubtedly in this Hebraic sense that the original Jewish disciples of Jesus understood and used the term. Only later, when the term entered into the Gentile world, did the phrase carry the idea of divinity. Roman and Greek mythology was filled with the offspring of the gods, who were known as sons of God. Hercules (Heracles) was the son of the high God Zeus (Jupiter). Most importantly, in the first century Caesar was called the Son of God.

When Jesus was born, Caesar Augustus was worshiped as the Son of God. During Jesus' lifetime there was a temple to Caesar Augustus at Caesarea Philippi. According to the gospels, this is the location where Peter professed Jesus as "the Son of the living God!" The geography of Peter's profession of faith was no accident. The Gospel writers were declaring that Jesus - not Caesar - was the true Son of God. In addition, the coin that Jesus used to make his point about paying taxes to Caesar was the "tribute penny," which had an image of Caesar Tiberius and words that described him as the Son of the divine Augustus. (Matthew 22:15-22)

To call Jesus the Son of God in Roman Palestine was a political statement. To claim to be the Son of God at that time and place was to claim to be a king. It was exactly that charge that was raised at his trial by the Sanhedrin. (Luke 22:69-71) It was equivalent to the charge brought before Pilate that Jesus was the king of Israel. (Matthew 27:11; Luke 23:3)

As time went on, it became necessary for Christians to distinguish Jesus from all the other sons of God in scripture and in the Roman world. Christ became "the only begotten Son." (First used in the Gospel of John, written at the end of the first century). The Greek term used here (monogenēs, μονογενὴς) meant "one of a kind, one and only." This was a theological statement that identified Jesus, not as a pagan demigod or an earthly monarch, but as the unique divine Son equal to God the Father. Later Jesus would be called "God the Son" and included as part of the Trinity. In this way the human Jesus came to be God the Son.

NO ONE UNDERSTANDS THE TRINITY

The doctrine of the Trinity distinguishes Christianity from other monotheistic religions, such as Judaism and Islam. For Christians the concept of one God in three persons is very important, yet it is also very confusing. When you think about it, the

Trinity does not make sense. No one understands it, not even your pastor.

The doctrine of the Trinity came into existence as a consequence of believing that Christ was divine. Christians believed that Jesus was divine in the same way that God the Father is divine. Yet Christians were loath to worship two Gods. It smacked of polytheism, not to mention the heresy of Marcionism. Add the Holy Spirit into the mix and Christianity seems to worship three gods - tritheism. (That is what Muslims accuse Christians of believing.)

The doctrine of the Trinity came out of the spiritual experience of early Christians. In addition to the God of the Old Testament, they also experienced Christ as God and the Spirit as God. Yet there could only be one God according to the Hebrew Scriptures. "Hear O Israel, the Lord your God, the Lord is one." (Deuteronomy 6:4) So they were forced into the untenable position of saying that God was both three and one, even though that statement was logically self-contradictory. The Father, Christ and the Spirit were all God, and they were also one God.

Christians had painted themselves into a theological corner. After repeated attempts by theologians to resolve the problem (all declared heresy), they simply gave up and declared that the Trinity was true, even though it didn't make sense. It is a mystery! A paradox! Actually it was just a problem they could not solve. Instead of abandoning the doctrine as untenable, they declared it to be true by fiat.

Christians have been trying to explain it ever since. Usually their attempts fall into some form of modalism, which was condemned as heresy by orthodox Christianity. Modalism, historically known as Sabellianism or Patripassianism, taught that the names of the Trinity refer to three modes or aspects of God, not distinct and coexisting persons, as in the orthodox understanding.

I have often heard ministers use the analogy of water to explain the Trinity. H_2O can be liquid, solid, or gas, depending on the temperature. Yet it is one substance. So – the reasoning goes – is God. A priest gave this explanation to Bill Maher in his controversial film *Religulous*, while standing on the grounds of the Vatican. Even that avowed atheist was impressed at the analogy. But it is modalism, in which the persons of the Trinity are different modes of God. Heresy hides in plain sight, even at the Vatican!

Another analogy is the relational one. The Trinity is like a man who is a father, a husband, and a son. He is a father to his children, a husband to his wife, and a son to this father. So is the Trinity! The problem is that such a God is one person playing different roles;

he is not three persons. This is also a form of modalism. I once heard a pastor use the same type of analogy by describing himself as a pastor, a custodian, and a school bus driver. So is God! No one seemed to notice that he was likening himself to God, not to mention calling God a janitor!

In a well-intentioned attempt to use gender inclusive language, some pastors refer to the Trinity as "Creator, Redeemer, Sustainer." But those titles describe functions or operations. That is classic modalism. It could easily degenerate into a tag-team trinity. The Father starts off by creating, the Son redeems, and the Spirit finishes up by sustaining. That is clearly not the biblical description of God.

One of the worst Trinitarian analogies is attributed to Saint Patrick. In evangelizing the Emerald Isle, he used the shamrock as a preaching illustration. The Trinity, he is reported to have said, is a like a three-leaf clover. The three pedals are the three persons of the trinity. Together they make one whole God.

Unfortunately that is just an Irish form of modalism. Each of the "persons" is one third God; together they equal one whole God. A similar analogy is an egg. The trinity is likened to the shell, white, and yolk of an egg. Together they comprise one God. That is one rotten egg and one more example of the same old heresy.

As the early Christians knew, the Trinity can be experienced but not described. C. S. Lewis comes the closest to this original intent in *Mere Christianity*:

> What I mean is this. An ordinary simple Christian kneels down to say his prayers. He is trying to get into touch with God. But if he is a Christian he knows that what is prompting him to pray is also God: God, so to speak, inside him. But he also knows that all his real knowledge of God comes through Christ, the Man who was God — that Christ is standing beside him, helping him to pray, praying for him. You see what is happening. God is the thing to which he is praying — the goal he is trying to reach. God is also the thing inside him which is pushing him on — the motive power. God is also the road or bridge along which he is being pushed to that goal. So that the whole threefold life of the three-personal Being is actually going on in that ordinary little bedroom where an ordinary man is saying his prayers. The man is being caught up into the higher kinds of life — what I called Zoe or spiritual life: he is being pulled into God, by God, while still remaining himself.[48]

Another thing your pastor will not tell you is that the Trinity is not in the Bible. The terms Father, Son, and Holy Spirit are found in the Bible. There are even a few places where the three words (or something similar) are found together. The most famous example is the Great Commission of Matthew 28:19, where Jesus commands his apostles to baptize all nations "in the name of the Father and of the Son and of the Holy Spirit." But nowhere is there any attempt in the Bible to define these names as three equally divine persons of one unified Godhead.

The doctrine of the Trinity, as we know it today in all its glorious confusion, originated in the third century by Tertullian. He was the first theologian to use the term "Trinity." He was also the first to use the words "person" and "substance" to explain the Father, Son, and Holy Spirit. It has been all downhill ever since. Christianity would have been better off if he had just left it as a description of Christian experience of instead of trying to theologize it.

WHAT MUST I DO TO BE SAVED?

The good news of the gospel is salvation. Salvation comes through Jesus Christ – his life, death, and resurrection. That is the message of early Christianity, and it is repeated in the Nicene Creed. Generally speaking, the various forms of early Christianity – expect for Gnosticism – agreed about what one is saved from and saved for. One was saved from the consequences of human sin – death and condemnation – and one was saved for eternal life. For that reason the Nicene Creed did not feel the need to elaborate upon the issue of salvation. The Chalcedonian creed does not address it at all.

Later there was much disagreement about salvation. The Protestant Reformation, which prompted the Council of Trent, centered on the relationship between faith and works in salvation. The relationship between faith and works was also important in earliest Christianity, as evidenced in the New Testament book of Acts, the letters of Paul and the Letter of James. The consensus of early orthodox Christianity is that salvation came through faith in Jesus Christ, and not by doing the works of the Law.

The Book of Acts purports to record the preaching of Peter and Paul, albeit from the orthodox perspective. It says that on the Day of Pentecost, fifty days after Jesus resurrection and only ten days after his ascension, Peter stood before a crowd in Jerusalem and proclaimed the gospel. He ended his message with the words, "Let all the house of Israel therefore know for certain that God has made him both Lord and Christ, this Jesus whom you crucified." (Acts 2:36) The story continues:

> Now when they heard this they were cut to the heart, and said to Peter and the rest of the apostles, "Brothers, what shall we do?" And Peter said to them, "Repent and be baptized every one of you in the name of Jesus Christ for the

forgiveness of your sins, and you will receive the gift of the Holy Spirit. For the promise is for you and for your children and for all who are far off, everyone whom the Lord our God calls to himself." And with many other words he bore witness and continued to exhort them, saying, "Save yourselves from this crooked generation." So those who received his word were baptized, and there were added that day about three thousand souls. (Acts 2:27-41)

This was just the beginning of similar preaching. The Book of Acts is a treasure trove of examples of orthodox Christian preaching, often accompanied by miracles that testified to the legitimacy of the message. Salvation and healing was always done in the name of Jesus and accomplished through faith.

When Phillip "preached Jesus" to the Ethiopian eunuch, the African responded in faith and was immediately baptized. According to Acts (as embellished by later orthodox editors by the addition of verse 37), "Then Philip opened his mouth, and beginning at this Scripture, preached Jesus to him. Now as they went down the road, they came to some water. And the eunuch said, 'See, here is water. What hinders me from being baptized?' Then Philip said, 'If you believe with all your heart, you may.' And he answered and said, 'I believe that Jesus Christ is the Son of God.' So he commanded the chariot to stand still. And both Philip and the eunuch went down into the water, and he baptized him." (Acts 8:35-38)

All it takes is faith in Jesus. Peter preached to Gentiles saying, "Whoever believes in him shall receive remission of sins," and the Holy Spirit immediately fell upon his hearers, not even waiting for baptism. (Acts 10:43-44) When Paul and Silas preached to the Philippian jailer, he responded, "Sirs, what must I do to be saved?" Their response was simply, "Believe on the Lord Jesus Christ, and you will be saved, you and your household." (Acts 16:31) The whole family was baptized that same night. The message of orthodox books such as Acts is clear: salvation is by faith in Jesus Christ. That is all that is needed.

Today if you asked the average evangelical or fundamentalist – or even mainline Protestant – how one is saved, you would get a similar answer. One is saved through faith in Christ. These days it would be framed in relational and experiential language. They would say that one has to have a personal relationship with Jesus, invite Jesus into your heart, or be born again.

If you asked a trained pastor, you would probably get a more theological answer. One is saved by the grace of God through faith in Christ. "By grace alone, by faith alone, in Christ alone." One is not saved by doing good deeds, except insofar as they are spiritual fruit that give evidence that a spiritual rebirth has happened in the person's life. This is the Protestant principle of justification by faith, which goes all the way back to the apostle Paul, and was rediscovered by Martin Luther.

That is not the way it always was. Neither Jesus nor the original apostles would have recognized such a gospel. Nor do all people today believe this theological formula. According to Barna's "The State of the Church 2016," even though 73% of the US population identify as Christian, most (55%) agree that if a person is generally good, or does good enough things for others during their life, they will earn a place in heaven, regardless of their faith.[49]

A 2016 Pew Research Center poll, taken for the 500th anniversary of the Protestant Reformation, agrees. It shows that over half of U.S. Protestants (52%) say both good deeds and faith are necessary for salvation, a historically Catholic position. The other half (46%) say that faith alone is needed for salvation.[50]

Jesus did not teach the orthodox doctrine of salvation by faith alone. Jesus believed in the importance of keeping the Jewish Law. In Matthew's gospel Jesus is pictured as a new Moses giving a new Law. He said in his Sermon on the Mount, "Do not think that I have come to abolish the Law or the

Prophets; I have not come to abolish them but to fulfill them. For truly, I say to you, until heaven and earth pass away, not an iota, not a dot, will pass from the Law until all is accomplished. Therefore whoever relaxes one of the least of these commandments and teaches others to do the same will be called least in the kingdom of heaven, but whoever does them and teaches them will be called great in the kingdom of heaven. For I tell you, unless your righteousness exceeds that of the scribes and Pharisees, you will never enter the kingdom of heaven." (Matthew 5:17-20)

Jesus goes on to describe how his followers are to exceed Pharisaic righteousness. For the next 28 verses, Jesus quotes the Law and then proclaims a stricter standard than the Mosaic Law. Instead of murder, his new law forbids anger. Instead of adultery, the problem is lust. The Law allows divorce; Jesus forbids it. In place of bearing false witness, Jesus forbids swearing under oath at all. Instead of an eye for an eye, Jesus instructs his followers to turn the other cheek. Instead of loving your neighbor, he advocates loving your enemies. He sums up his new law with this command: "Therefore you shall be perfect, just as your Father in heaven is perfect." (Matthew 5:48)

Is keeping the Law the basis for entering eternal life? It appears so. A rich young ruler came to Jesus and asked, "What must I do to inherit eternal life?"

This would have been the perfect opportunity for Jesus to preach the evangelical gospel and say, "Believe in me and you shall have eternal life." But he did not say that. Instead he said, "If you want to enter into life, keep the commandments." (Matthew 19:17) When the man said he had kept the commandments since he was a boy, Jesus had another chance to set the man straight and proclaim the gospel of salvation by grace through faith. But instead he gives him a stricter standard. He tells him to sell all his possessions and follow him. Then he would have "treasure in heaven." (Matthew 19:16-22; Mark 10:17-27)

Jesus' view of salvation is not the Christian gospel of today. Every pastor who has studied the Bible knows that. Indeed this fact is available to every Christian who takes the time to carefully read everything that Jesus taught on the subject. Don't take my word for it. Read the synoptic gospels for yourself. Most of Jesus' words speak of good deeds as the standard by which one gains entrance to heaven.

In some passages it appears as if Jesus – or the writer of the Gospel of Matthew – is combatting those who advocate a wider path of salvation by faith alone. He calls them false prophets, and says it is not enough to be religious and believe in him as "Lord." It is necessary to do the will of God. He ends his Sermon on the Mount with such words.

Enter by the narrow gate. For the gate is wide and the way is easy that leads to destruction, and those who enter by it are many. For the gate is narrow and the way is hard that leads to life, and those who find it are few.

Beware of false prophets, who come to you in sheep's clothing but inwardly are ravenous wolves. You will recognize them by their fruits. Are grapes gathered from thornbushes, or figs from thistles? So, every healthy tree bears good fruit, but the diseased tree bears bad fruit. A healthy tree cannot bear bad fruit, nor can a diseased tree bear good fruit. Every tree that does not bear good fruit is cut down and thrown into the fire. Thus you will recognize them by their fruits.

Not everyone who says to me, 'Lord, Lord,' will enter the kingdom of heaven, but the one who does the will of my Father who is in heaven. On that day many will say to me, 'Lord, Lord, did we not prophesy in your name, and cast out demons in your name, and do many mighty works in your name?' And then will I declare to them, 'I never knew you; depart from me, you workers of lawlessness.' (Matthew 7:13-23)

Many of Jesus' parables directly address his standard for gaining entrance into the Kingdom of

Heaven. Not all of his parables address the topic of salvation. But when they do, good works are usually the criteria used.

In the parable of the Sheep and the Goats (Matthew 25:31-46), the standard used for separating the saved from the lost is whether they welcomed strangers, fed the hungry, gave water to the thirsty, clothed the naked, and visited prisoners. The King's standard is summed up in this rule: "As you did it to one of the least of these my brothers, you did it to me." There is no mention of faith.

In the parable of the Rich Man and Lazarus (Luke 16:19-31), the rich man finds himself in hell because he ignored the pleas of the poor sitting at his gate, who only desired to be fed with the crumbs that fell from the rich man's table. The rich man begs Abraham to send someone to warn his brothers, so they would not end up in hell also. But Abraham says that they have already been warned – through the Law. "But Abraham said, 'They have Moses and the Prophets; let them hear them.' And he said, 'No, father Abraham, but if someone goes to them from the dead, they will repent.' He said to him, 'If they do not hear Moses and the Prophets, neither will they be convinced if someone should rise from the dead.'" (Luke 16:29-31) Apparently the Law is sufficient for salvation.

Some parables mention repentance and belief, such as the parable of the Two Sons. (Matthew 21:28-32) But even then the chief standard is not just knowing what is right, but doing it. In the parable of the Pharisee and the Tax Collector (Luke 18:9-14), Jesus makes it clear that legalistic observance of the Law – as practiced by his nemeses the Pharisees - is not sufficient. There must be genuine and heartfelt repentance, but again there is no mention of faith.

There are many parables where Jesus teaches the importance of being ready for the Kingdom (The Ten Virgins, Matthew 25:1-13; the Two men and Two women, Matthew 24:36-41; the Wise Servant, Matthew 24:25-51; the thief in the night; Matthew 24:42-44). For the apocalyptic preacher Jesus, it was very important that his followers were on the lookout and prepared for the coming Kingdom. But there is no mention of faith.

"Therefore, stay awake, for you do not know on what day your Lord is coming. But know this, that if the master of the house had known in what part of the night the thief was coming, he would have stayed awake and would not have let his house be broken into. Therefore you also must be ready, for the Son of Man is coming at an hour you do not expect." (Matthew 24:42-44)

There are parables that stress grace, such as the parables of the lost coin, the lost sheep and the lost sons (the prodigal son) of Luke 15. Only one of these three involve any type of repentance, and even then the motivation of the prodigal son is dubious. The coin obviously does not have faith, not does the sheep. The theme of all three stories is the grace of God, not the faith of humans.

We could go through all the parables of Jesus looking for the orthodox doctrine of salvation by faith and never find it. In the synoptic Gospels, which are the earliest and most reliable sources for the teachings of Jesus, there is no evidence that such a doctrine was taught by Jesus or known by his original disciples. Not until we come to the Gospel of John, written at least sixty years after Jesus' death, do we find faith in Jesus as the Son of God as the means for gaining entrance to heaven.

It is fine to believe in the doctrine of salvation by faith. All my life I have preached a gospel of God's saving grace through faith in Jesus Christ. But let us not add lies to our faith. Let us not pretend that Jesus taught this or that his original twelve disciples believed it. The way taught by Jesus was a very different path of salvation. It was a Jewish gospel that taught that salvation comes through strict obedience to the will of God, as well as preparation and expectation for the imminent coming of the Kingdom of God.

In like manner the gospel preached by evangelical and fundamentalist Christianity today is different than any taught in scripture. Correct doctrine has become an essential ingredient for salvation in today's popular Christianity. Salvation involves believing the right ideas. The biblical faith in Christ has been replaced by faith in theology, with some emotion thrown in.

Originally Christian faith was defined as trust in a person – the person of Christ. Today it is not enough for a person to trust in Jesus. One must adhere to a proper understanding of Jesus, as well as a host of other doctrines. One's eternal salvation is dependent upon holding correct Christian ideas. No longer can one simply respond to the call of Jesus to "follow me." Now one much pass a theological litmus test before being admitted into the band of disciples.

This is salvation by knowledge, which is an intellectualized form of Gnosticism. But it is not as vibrant and alive as the early Gnostic forms of Christianity. In the case of evangelical and fundamentalist Christianity, salvation is not gained through experiential knowledge of Christ alone. It must be accompanied by doctrinal knowledge. We are saved – at least in part – by mentally acknowledging certain carefully defined dogmas. Modern Christianity is just another variation of old heretical themes. Because modern Christians do not know Church history, they are doomed to repeat it.

Like all sects, modern evangelicals and fundamentalists are convinced they alone are right. Theirs is the one true faith. They possess the true gospel handed down from the beginning by Jesus and the apostles. They are the only ones who truly understand the Bible. They see it as is their God-given task to share this truth with others and win the world for Christ. People's eternal destinies are on the line. Listen to the spiel of a Mormon or a Jehovah's Witness, and you will hear basically the same approach as a Christian fundamentalist. It is ignorance and delusion. To adapt Lord Acton's famous maxim: Religion deludes, and absolute religion deludes absolutely.

The faith described by the apostle Paul and the Gospel of John was trust in Christ; it was relational. Paul did not say, "Believe in the Trinity, the inerrancy of scripture, six literal days of creation, the full humanity and divinity of Jesus Christ, and you shall be saved." He said, "Believe in the Lord Jesus Christ and you shall be saved."

John did not write, "For God so loved the world that he sent his only begotten Son that whoever believes in the Nicene Creed, should not perish but have everlasting life." Christians had faith in a person, not a theological system.

Modern Christianity's concept of salvation has become a superficial intellectual assent to beliefs about Christ combined with sentimental music and a romantic attachment to Jesus. It has none of the depth and vitality of the early Christian message.

THE SECOND COMING DIDN'T HAPPEN

"Jesus is coming soon!" That is the message I heard repeatedly after becoming a Christian during college in the 1970's. [51] There was a spirit of anticipation in the air. Christ could come at any time! Some members of the Christian Fellowship on our campus held "rapture drills," in which they stood on a hilltop and leapt into the air. They were practicing for that glorious day when, according to the Bible, "Christ will descend" and believers on earth "will be caught up in the clouds to meet the Lord in the air." (I Thessalonians 4:17 NLT)

It was an exciting time to be a Christian. It seemed like Biblical prophecies were being fulfilled every day. *The Late, Great Planet Earth* by Hal Lindsey had recently been published in 1970. He interpreted Revelation in the light of newspaper headlines. It was all coming together in our lifetime! The European

Union was on the way to becoming the revived Roman Empire. The Soviet Union was on the verge of invading Israel in what Revelation referred to as the War of Gog and Magog. The Antichrist was already alive and walking the earth!

Lindsey predicted the Second Coming of Christ in 1988, calculating it as forty years (one generation) from the establishment of the modern state of Israel. We were looking forward to the day of our Lord's return. In his subsequent work *The 1980s: Countdown to Armageddon*, Lindsey wrote: "the decade of the 1980s could very well be the last decade of history as we know it." How blessed we were to be living in the end times!

As the years went on – and 1988 came and went without any sign of Jesus – I learned that Lindsay was not the first or the last Christian teacher to set a date for the Second Coming ... and be wrong. Revelation is the favorite stomping ground of date-setters for the end of the world. There is no shortage of people who think they can decipher every detail of Revelation and are obsessed with producing intricate color-coded charts of the future.

Throughout history people have set dates for the future coming of Christ. Augustine dated it at AD 1000, Joachim de Fiore at 1266, and Martin Luther at 1558. William Miller of the Adventists got very specific; he predicted Christ's return on October 22, 1844. When it didn't happen, his followers called the nonevent "The Great Disappointment." The Seventh Day Adventists later explained that Miller was only partly wrong. What had happened on October 22 was not Jesus' return to earth, as Miller thought, but the start of Jesus' final work of atonement in heaven, the cleansing of the heavenly sanctuary, which leads up to the Second Coming.

Charles Russell of the Jehovah's Witnesses predicted the Second Coming to occur in 1914. When that year passed without incident, they followed the Adventists' lead. They declared that they had the date right, but it had been an invisible coming of Christ. Jesus just changed locations in heaven instead of returning to earth. John Wesley, the founder of Methodism, in his commentary on Revelation strongly suggested (but wisely did not definitely predict) that the end was coming in 1836. Herbert W. Armstrong of the Worldwide Church of God set the date for 1975.

In more recent decades Christian radio broadcaster Harold Camping determined the Lord's return to be in 1994. When that date fell through, he revised his calculations and came to a corrected date of May 21, 2011. Billboards were erected around the country warning people to be ready. When May 22 dawned, he changed it to October 21, 2011. The billboards were amended, only to be dismantled when November arrived without a sign of Christ.

Picking up on the Y2K hysteria at the turn of the millennium, many people predicted Christ's return around the year 2000. These included Christian celebrities like Jerry Falwell and Ed Dobson, who followed in the footsteps of earlier predictors of 2000 such as Isaac Newton and Edgar Cayce.

In 2008, Christian ministers Mark Biltz and John Hagee began proclaiming the Blood Moon Prophecy, which linked Christ's return to a series of four consecutive lunar eclipses, which coincided with Jewish holidays. The date of Jesus' return would be the lunar eclipse on September 28, 2015. Once again, Jesus did not appear in the clouds. Picking up on the media fascination with the Mayan calendar, televangelist Jack Van Impe predicted 2012 as the date. He now wisely teaches that we cannot know the exact date.

If you think you may have missed out on the fun, don't be alarmed. There are more prophecy teachers linking the Book of Revelation to modern events in Europe, Russia, China, the United States, and the Middle East. Ronald Weinland of the Worldwide Church of God, who calls himself "the last apostle to God's Church before Christ returns to establish God's Kingdom" has set a date of June 8, 2019. Those of a more occult inclination can turn to the writings of 20th century psychic and astrologer Jeane Dixon, who predicted that Armageddon would take place in 2020 and Jesus would return between 2020 and 2037.

What many Christians may not realize – and your pastor has likely not told you - is that this pattern of prediction and disappointment goes back to New Testament times. Jesus himself predicted a date for his Second Coming. He said, "For the Son of Man is going to come with his angels in the glory of his Father, and then he will repay each person according to what he has done. Truly, I say to you, there are some standing here who will not taste death until they see the Son of Man coming in his kingdom." (Matthew 16:28)

In another place he said, "For whoever is ashamed of me and of my words, of him will the Son of Man be ashamed when he comes in his glory and the glory of the Father and of the holy angels. But I tell you truly, there are some standing here who will not taste death until they see the kingdom of God." (Luke 9:26-27)

Those prophecies are pretty clear. Jesus believed that an apocalyptic figure called the Son of Man (which the early Christians assumed was Jesus himself) would return and usher in his kingdom within the lifetimes of those who heard him speak those words. When that generation of Christians eventually passed away without any appearance of the Savior, it created a crisis in the Christian community.

Was Jesus mistaken? Was he (God forbid!) a false prophet? That is what the Old Testament test for a false prophet seem to indicate. "If what a prophet proclaims in the name of the LORD does not take place or come true, that is a message the LORD has not spoken. That prophet has spoken presumptuously, so do not be alarmed." (Deuteronomy 18:22)

The present ending of the Gospel of John was written to address this crisis of faith. There was a prophecy spoken by Jesus, which was well-known to the church in Ephesus. It taught specifically that the Apostle John would not die before Christ returned. Then the unthinkable happened. John, the last of the original twelve apostles, died! How could that be explained? Was everything they believed about Christ and his Second Coming wrong? To avert a crisis, the final editor of John's gospel added a scene to explain the apparent contradiction.

When Peter saw him, he said to Jesus, "Lord, what about this man?" Jesus said to him, "If it is my will that he remain until I come, what is that to you? You follow me!" So the saying spread abroad among the brothers that this disciple was not to die; yet Jesus did not say to him that he was not to die, but, "If it is my will that he remain until I come, what is that to you?" (John 21:21-23)

Was Jesus mistaken? No, explains the editor of John's gospel. People misheard what Jesus said. It was all a big misunderstanding. Jesus never really said he would return within the lifetime of John. Whew!

The belief in the imminent return of Christ is taught in the Book of Revelation. Revelation starts off with these words: "The revelation of Jesus Christ, which God gave him to show to his servants the things that must soon take place. He made it known by sending his angel to his servant John, who bore witness to the word of God and to the testimony of Jesus Christ, even to all that he saw. Blessed is the one who reads aloud the words of this prophecy, and blessed are those who hear, and who keep what is written in it, for the time is near." (Revelation 1:1-3) Revelation describes things that "must soon take place" "for the time is near." The book of Revelation ends on the same note. Jesus says, "Surely I am coming soon." Then the final editor of the book adds, "Amen. Come, Lord Jesus!" (Revelation 22:20)

First century Christians believed that Jesus would return in their lifetimes. The apostle Paul expected the imminent return of the Lord in his lifetime and that of his readers. "For the Lord himself will descend from heaven with a cry of command, with the voice of an archangel, and with the sound of the trumpet of God. And the dead in Christ will rise first. Then we who are alive, who are left, will be caught up together with them in the clouds to meet the Lord in the air, and so we will always be with the Lord." (I Thessalonians 4:16-17) Paul expects himself and some of his readers to be alive when Christ returns.

When the last of the original generation of Christians died, it created a problem for early Christianity. This dilemma is addressed in the pseudonymous Second Letter of Peter, a New Testament book written about the same time as John's gospel. This books describes "scoffers" who point out the delay in Christ's return and conclude that he is never coming. It says:

> This is now the second letter that I am writing to you, beloved. In both of them I am stirring up your sincere mind by way of reminder, that you should remember the predictions of the holy prophets and the commandment of the Lord and Savior through your apostles, knowing this first of all, that scoffers will come in the last days with scoffing, following their own sinful desires. They will say, "Where is the promise of his coming? For ever since the fathers fell asleep, all things are

continuing as they were from the beginning of creation." (2 Peter 3:1-4)

The solution to the failure of Christ's promised imminent return was to reinterpret what the word "soon" means. It turns out that "soon" does not mean what we think is does. Soon isn't soon. (It reminds me of Rudy Giuliani's August 2018 statement that "truth isn't truth.") God has his own timing. He does not measure time like we do.

As Second Peter goes on to say: "But do not overlook this one fact, beloved, that with the Lord one day is as a thousand years, and a thousand years as one day. The Lord is not slow to fulfill his promise as some count slowness, but is patient toward you, not wishing that any should perish, but that all should reach repentance." (2 Peter 3:8-9) Problem solved. God uses a different clock.

The same type of crisis occurred after the destruction of Jerusalem, which was predicted by Jesus. In his famous Olivet Discourse, Jesus predicted the desecration of the temple and the compete destruction of Jerusalem. That came to pass in 70 AD, within that generation, just as Jesus predicted. (Matthew 24:1-27; cf. Mark 13:1-24; Luke 21:5-24) But Jesus goes on to say that the destruction of Jerusalem will be immediately followed by apocalyptic events including the Second Coming.

Immediately after the tribulation of those days the sun will be darkened, and the moon will not give its light, and the stars will fall from heaven, and the powers of the heavens will be shaken. Then will appear in heaven the sign of the Son of Man, and then all the tribes of the earth will mourn, and they will see the Son of Man coming on the clouds of heaven with power and great glory. And he will send out his angels with a loud trumpet call, and they will gather his elect from the four winds, from one end of heaven to the other. "From the fig tree learn its lesson: as soon as its branch becomes tender and puts out its leaves, you know that summer is near. So also, when you see all these things, you know that he is near, at the very gates. Truly, I say to you, this generation will not pass away until all these things take place. Heaven and earth will pass away, but my words will not pass away. (Matthew 24:29-35; cf. Mark 13:24-31, Luke 21:25-28)

But those events did not happen "immediately after the tribulation of those days." All the gospel writers knew that because they wrote a decade or more after the capture of Jerusalem by the Roman armies in 70 AD. So a disclaimer is added in the very next verse. "But concerning that day and hour no one knows, not even the angels of heaven, nor the Son, but the Father only." (Matthew 24:36; cf. Mark 13:32)

Those words were the gospel writers' way of explaining why Jesus did not return immediately after the destruction of Jerusalem. They were admitting that Jesus did not know everything. Didn't the gospel admit that Jesus "grew in wisdom?" (Luke 2:52) The exact timing of his return was one of those areas that Jesus admitted he did not know.

In fact the writing of all four gospels was prompted by the realization that Christ was not coming within their lifetimes to set up his kingdom. Therefore they better preserve Jesus' words and deeds in writing so that future generations would know about him. We have the gospels of the New Testament only because Jesus did not return in a timely manner.

Jesus got the timing of the Second Coming wrong, and Christians have been getting it wrong ever since. Christians need to take that error into consideration in their Christology. If Jesus was mistaken about something like this, then maybe he was wrong about another important topic: hell.

JESUS WAS A HELLFIRE PREACHER

Hell is not a popular topic these days, even in evangelical churches.[52] The doctrine has fallen on hard times. It is too mean-spirited and hateful for our age, and the church today does not want to come across as hateful. But no matter how you spin it, hell is not nice, and the church wants to present a nice face. So hell is down-played. Preachers do not want to be accused of hate speech. It is bad for business. It would keep people away from church, and the whole purpose of preaching is to bring people to Christ and into his Church.

Preachers and churches who boldly warn people about the danger of hell, such as the controversial Westboro Baptist Church that pickets funerals with signs reading "You're Going to Hell" and "God Hates You," are vilified in the press. Other Baptist preachers are quick to distance themselves from these fellow Baptists, even though they may actually agree with them theologically. Strategically it is smarter for Baptists to present a kinder, gentler face to the public.

Paige Patterson, the recently ousted president of Southwestern Baptist Theological Seminary, said, "You can traverse the entire United States on any given Sunday morning, and you very probably will not hear a sermon on the judgement of God or eternal punishment." He adds, "Evangelicals have voted by the silence of their voices that they either do not believe in [the doctrine of Hell] or else no longer have the courage and conviction to stand and say anything about it."[53]

Your pastor probably won't tell you that the New Testament teaches that hell is the eternal destination for the vast majority of human beings. The Old Testament afterlife consisted only of a shadowy existence called Sheol for everyone. But by New Testament times the afterlife had become much more vivid. It had expanded to two departments – reward for the righteous and punishment for the damned.

That is why evangelical and fundamentalist Christians still believe in hell, even though they may not advertise it as openly as in the past. Their belief in hell is wrapped up with the authority and inspiration of Holy Scripture. For conservative Christians the Bible is the inerrant Word of God. Whatever the Bible teaches must be accepted without question or compromise. As "America's pastor" Saddleback Church minister Rick Warren tweeted, "I believe in hell because Jesus says it's real & he knows more about it than anyone."

He's right. Jesus preached hell. In fact Jesus is the biggest hellfire preacher in the Bible. Michael Allen Rogers, author of *What Happens After I Die?* calls Jesus "the Great Theologian of Hell." No one in the Bible speaks more about the infernal regions than Jesus.

Jesus did not invent the concept of hell. The idea came from the Greeks and had been absorbed into Jewish culture and religion by the time Jesus was born. Palestine was ruled during the second century BC by the Greek Seleucid Empire. At that time Hellenistic culture seeped deeply into the Jewish psyche. It is no accident that the New Testament was written in Greek, with only a smattering of Hebrew and Aramaic words, which were the languages spoken by Jesus and his apostles. With the Greek language came the Greek worldview.

Part of that worldview was the afterlife, including otherworldly punishment and suffering. Sisyphus pushed a boulder up a hill forever. Tantalus was cursed with eternal thirst. Prometheus had his liver eaten daily. Such otherworldly retributions fit nicely into the Jewish belief in divine justice. If there was no justice in this life, then at least there will be justice in the afterlife. Heaven and hell provided that justice.

Christianity borrowed hell from the Greek mythological place of punishment called Tartarus, a Greek word that is used for hell in the New Testament. (2 Peter 2:4) In his *Gorgias*, Plato said that souls were judged after death and those who received punishment were sent to Tartarus. In Greek mythology, Tartarus was an abyss used as a dungeon of torment located within the larger territory of Hades, which was like the Old Testament Sheol. Jesus took this idea of hell and made it his own. He called it Gehenna, naming it after the Jerusalem city dump in the Valley of Hinnom, which continuously burned the rubbish of the Jerusalemites.

In the centuries after Jesus, the Christian hell became more like the Dantean inferno we are familiar with. The second century Apocalypse of Peter (which almost made it into the New Testament; it is mentioned in the Muratorian fragment, which contains the oldest surviving list of New Testament books) is a tour of hell given by the apostle Peter, reminiscent of Dante's tour led by Virgil.

In the Apocalypse of Peter each type of sinner gets his just reward. Blasphemers are hung by their tongues. Adulterers are suspended over a boiling lake – women by their hair and men by their feet. Murderers are in a pit of venomous snakes and creeping things. Women who had abortions are buried to their neck in blood and gore; their aborted children torment them with flames of fire. Usurers are mired in a lake of muck and blood. Disobedient slaves chew their own tongues and are tortured with eternal fire forever. In fact Dante borrowed his visions of hell from a similar apocryphal account, the third century Apocalypse of Paul, which purports to be the vision of Paul of Tarsus mentioned in 2 Corinthians 12:1-7.

The Christian hell got its start with Jesus. What exactly did Jesus teach about hell? He says it is a place of bodily suffering. He said, "If your right eye causes you to sin, pluck it out and cast it from you; for it is more profitable for you that one of your members perish, than for your whole body to be cast into hell. And if your right hand causes you to sin, cut it off and cast it from you; for it is more profitable for you that one of your members perish, than for your whole body to be cast into hell." (Matthew 5:29-30) "And do not fear those who kill the body but cannot kill the soul. But rather fear Him who is able to destroy both soul and body in hell." (Matthew 10:28)

In parallel passages Jesus make it clear that hell is a place of eternal fire as well as physical pain. "If your hand causes you to sin, cut it off. It is better for you to enter into life maimed, rather than having two hands, to go to hell, into the fire that shall never be quenched." (Mark 9:43) "And if your foot causes you to sin, cut it off. It is better for you to enter life lame, rather than having two feet, to be cast into hell, into the fire that shall never be quenched." (Mark 9:45) "And if your eye causes you to sin, pluck it out. It is better for you to enter the kingdom of God with one eye, rather than having two eyes, to be cast into hell fire." (Mark 9:47).

In other verses Jesus describes it as a fiery furnace. "The Son of Man will send his angels, and they will gather out of his kingdom all causes of sin and all law-breakers, and throw them into the fiery furnace.

In that place there will be weeping and gnashing of teeth. So it will be at the end of the age. The angels will come out and separate the evil from the righteous and throw them into the fiery furnace. In that place there will be weeping and gnashing of teeth." (Matthew 13:41-42, 49-50).

Alongside the hellfire imagery, Jesus also describes hell as a place of "outer darkness." "But the sons of the kingdom will be cast out into outer darkness. There will be weeping and gnashing of teeth." (Matthew 8:12) "Bind him hand and foot, take him away, and cast him into outer darkness; there will be weeping and gnashing of teeth." (Matthew 22:13, also Matthew 24:51, Matthew 25:30) Jesus' most iconic description of the afterlife is his story of the rich man and Lazarus. It is worth quoting in its entirety.

There was a certain rich man who was clothed in purple and fine linen and fared sumptuously every day. But there was a certain beggar named Lazarus, full of sores, who was laid at his gate, desiring to be fed with the crumbs which fell from the rich man's table. Moreover the dogs came and licked his sores. So it was that the beggar died, and was carried by the angels to Abraham's bosom. The rich man also died and was buried. And being in torments in Hades, he lifted up his eyes and saw Abraham afar off, and Lazarus in his bosom. "Then he cried and said, 'Father Abraham, have mercy on me, and send Lazarus that he may dip the tip of his finger in water and cool my tongue; for I am tormented in this flame.' But Abraham said, 'Son, remember that in your lifetime you received your good things, and likewise Lazarus evil things; but now he is comforted and you are tormented. And besides all this, between us and you there is a great gulf fixed, so that those who want to pass from here to you cannot, nor can those from there pass to us.' "Then he said, 'I beg you therefore, father, that you would send him to my father's house, for I have five brothers, that he may testify to them, lest they also come to this place of torment.' Abraham said to him, 'They have Moses and the prophets; let them hear them.' And he said, 'No, father Abraham; but if one goes to them from the dead, they will repent.' But he said to him, 'If they do not hear Moses and the prophets, neither will they be persuaded though one rise from the dead.' (Luke 16:19–31)

In this story Jesus depicts hell as a place of torment, which is in full sight of the pleasures of heaven. Furthermore those in heaven are prohibited by God from showing any mercy to the inhabitants of hell. Another famous teaching of Jesus about hell is found in the Parable of the Unforgiving Servant. It was told in response to Peter's question about forgiveness.

> Then Peter came to Him and said, "Lord, how often shall my brother sin against me, and I forgive him? Up to seven times?" Jesus said to him, "I do not say to you, up to seven times, but up to seventy times seven. Therefore the kingdom of heaven is like a certain king who wanted to settle accounts with his servants. And when he had begun to settle accounts, one was brought to him who owed him ten thousand talents. But as he was not able to pay, his master commanded that he be sold, with his wife and children and all that he had, and that payment be made. The servant therefore fell down before him, saying, 'Master, have patience with me, and I will pay you all.' Then the master of that servant was moved with compassion, released him, and forgave him the debt. "But that servant went out and found one of his fellow servants who owed him a hundred denarii; and he laid hands on him and took him by the throat, saying, 'Pay me what you owe!' So his fellow servant fell down at his feet and begged him, saying, 'Have patience with me, and I will pay you all.' And he would not, but went and threw him into prison till he should pay the debt. So when his fellow servants saw what had been done, they were very grieved, and came and told

their master all that had been done. Then his master, after he had called him, said to him, 'You wicked servant! I forgave you all that debt because you begged me. Should you not also have had compassion on your fellow servant, just as I had pity on you?' And his master was angry, and delivered him to the torturers until he should pay all that was due to him. "So My heavenly Father also will do to you if each of you, from his heart, does not forgive his brother his trespasses." (Matthew 18:21-35)

Jesus teaches that God will torture those who do not forgive. Isn't that contradictory? If we are to forgive, should not God also forgive? In any case, it is clear that for Jesus hell is a place of never-ending punishment. It is "hell, the unquenchable fire...where their worm does not die and the fire is not quenched." (Mark 9:48-49)

The Book of Revelation, which is presented not as the ideas of John but "the revelation of Jesus Christ" (Rev. 1:1), says of one who suffers this eternal punishment, "he also will drink the wine of God's wrath, poured full strength into the cup of his anger, and he will be tormented with fire and sulfur in the presence of the holy angels and in the presence of the Lamb. And the smoke of their torment goes up forever and ever, and they have no rest, day or night." (Revelation 14:9-11) The torture does not happen in some faraway dungeon but "in the presence of the holy angels and in the presence of the Lamb," who is Christ.

Imagine the worst torture chambers ever conceived by evil humans and multiply it by infinity and you have Jesus' teaching about hell. This portrait of Jesus as a fire-and-brimstone preacher does not sit well with Christians today. We prefer "gentle Jesus, meek and mild." We hang paintings in our churches depicting a kindly Jesus surrounded by little children or carrying a little lamb. You will not find any paintings in Protestant churches of Jesus sending people into the flames of eternal torment.

Christians have done a good job of rebranding Jesus. He is no longer the proclaimer of hell. He is now the teacher of unconditional love. God is Love! God – and Jesus – love the world and everyone in it. He would never permit – much less order – that anyone be tortured for all eternity.

Increasingly aware of the cognitive dissonance inherent in believing in a loving God who would create a literal eternal hell of endless suffering, Christians have downplayed hell in recent decades. It is simply not talked about much. It might scare away "seekers." You will seldom hear the topic preached in mainline Protestant churches, and or even in conservative churches.

In her book *Who Goes There? A Cultural History of Heaven and Hell,* Rebecca Price Janney traces this shift in attitude toward hell to the World War II era. During that war, religious leaders conducting the funerals of fallen soldiers often implied that dead American soldiers couldn't possibly be in hell because they'd already "been through hell" on the battlefield. The idea proffered comfort to grieving loved ones. Janney writes, "This caught on and persisted over the decades, and we saw it re-emerge strongly during the September 11, 2001 terrorist attacks: 'How could these dear people who died so tragically possibly go to hell?'"

Even evangelist Billy Graham, known for his fire and brimstone preaching early in his career, mellowed. During his sermon at the National Cathedral memorializing those who died on 9/11, he made the extraordinary – and completely unverifiable - claim that many who died in the twin towers went immediately to heaven. "And many of those people who died this past week are in heaven now. And they wouldn't want to come back. It's so glorious and so wonderful."

Though this is far from liberal universalism, Graham's words are also a far cry from Jesus pronouncement that "many are called, but few are chosen" and "wide is the gate and broad is the way that leads to destruction, and many enter through it.

But small is the gate and narrow the way that leads to life, and only a few find it."

Not content to sidestep the subject of hell, many Christians have sought to redefine it. Instead of describing it as a place of suffering and torment, hell is increasingly defined simply as "separation from God." In 1994 Christian apologist William Lane Craig debated atheist philosopher Ray Bradley at Simon Frasier University, Vancouver, British Columbia, Canada, on the topic "Can a Loving God Send People to Hell?" It is a very thorough examination of the arguments on both sides of the issue. In the debate Ray Bradley chides William Lane Craig for downplaying hell by using such terminology.

Bradley said, "Dr. Craig likes to talk about hell in such soothing terms as everlasting separation from God. This a favorite dodge of Christians. It makes our question sound rather like "Can a loving God send some of His children to Hawaii?" Think about it like this, and the answer seems obvious. Why not, if that is where some of them choose to go?" He continues, "Keeping Dr. Craig's biblical conservatism in mind, then, let's ask "How should we think of God's sending people to hell?" Not like Stalin sending people to exile in Siberia. It ought not even to be thought of as like Hitler sending people to the gas chambers of Auschwitz. For both of these are tame in comparison with the horror of being sent to hell."[54]

Still others have sought to demythologize hell. If hell as a postmortem destination is no longer viable, perhaps we can reinterpret it to apply to this earthly life. Perhaps hell is just a metaphor for human suffering and evil. We make our own hell in this life. Maybe that is what Jesus was really getting at! Is it possible that he was not really talking about the fate of the soul after death but about hell on earth? Hell would then be like Jean Paul Sartre's play "No Exit." As the famous line says, "hell is other people."

How would we demythologize hell? What could the symbol of hell possibly represent? It could be the suffering that we inflict upon ourselves and others. "War Is Hell" as General William Tecumseh Sherman so famously said. Who would deny that the Jewish holocaust was a form of hell, or Pol Pot's killing fields, or the prison camps of North Korea? The torture chambers of the Spanish Inquisition were earthly hells. Drug addiction is hell. Physical and sexual abuse is hell. There are certainly ample examples of serial killers who have made the lives of their victims hell. There is no shortage of examples of human devils who have made people's lives a living hell.

But when we try to apply the words of Scripture to these man-made hells, they do not ring true. Jesus was not talking about hells created by humans but hell created by his Heavenly Father. Hell is "prepared for the devil and his angels" but used to take revenge on human beings, as Jesus parable of the Sheep and Goats makes clear. (Matthew 25:31-46)

What loving parent sends – or even permits – his children to spend eternity in torment? As a father I would not wish terrible suffering on my worst enemy, much less my children, no matter how disobedient or rebellious they had been. As Jesus says, "If you then, who are evil, know how to give good gifts to your children, how much more will your Father who is in heaven give good things to those who ask him!" (Matthew 7:11)

But there is one other possibility. Maybe there is no hell. Maybe Christianity got it wrong. Perhaps it is a myth. Maybe Jesus was mistaken. After all he was human. Maybe he was all too human. Maybe it was his fallible human nature speaking those words about hell. He admitted that there were some things he did not know. When it came to the timing of his return and of the end of the age, Jesus said, "But concerning that day and hour no one knows, not even the angels of heaven, nor the Son, but the Father only." (Matthew 24:36)

On the other hand maybe the gospel writers got Jesus' words wrong. They misunderstood the words of Jesus and reported them incorrectly, as the end of John's gospel suggests about his second coming.

Maybe they put these words about hell in Jesus' mouth.

As disruptive as it would be to Christianity to admit that hell is a human construct and not a metaphysical reality, it is a better option than having a God who is an Eternal Torturer. Sure, we would have to tweak our understanding of scriptural authority and inspiration. But what is the alternative?

If Jesus really preached hell, and he was not mistaken or misquoted, then the consequences are disturbing. It means that Christians worship a God who created a place of eternal torment for the vast majority of the population of the earth. Hell is not just for Satan, his demons, and a few really bad people, such as Hitler, Stalin, Pol Pot, and other mass murderers. According to Jesus, most of the people who have ever lived are in hell. Only a few – a small percentage of humans - make it to heaven.

"Enter by the narrow gate. For the gate is wide and the way is easy that leads to destruction, and those who enter by it are many. For the gate is narrow and the way is hard that leads to life, and those who find it are few." (Matthew 7:13-14) Or as Jesus was fond of saying on many occasions, "Many are called, but few are chosen."

However you want to creatively interpret the words "many" and "few," it still means that a lot of people – billions and billions of them - are today suffering unspeakable torment for all eternity, while a blessed few enjoy the eternal bliss of heaven. That is what Jesus preached. I bet that is something your pastor hasn't told you.

.

6

WHAT YOUR PASTOR WON'T TELL YOU ABOUT CHRISTIAN ETHICS

Religion and ethics go together. There is no debate about that. Nearly every religion includes a set of ethical rules governing private and public behavior. On the other hand, it is up for debate whether religion makes people more ethical.

The promotion of public morality plays a large role in American religion, especially of the conservative and evangelical varieties. Conservative Christians banded together in the 1980's and called themselves the "Moral Majority," seeking to halt the moral decay of American society. Christians fervently defend the posting of the Ten Commandments on public property, arguing that these God-given laws are the foundation of a moral society, even though surveys show that most Christians do not keep them or even know them.[55]

God is considered to be the guardian of morality. If there is no God, there is no metaphysical basis for morality. As Dostoevsky wrote in *The Brothers Karamazov*, "If God does not exist, everything is permitted." There is an assumption among Christians that you have to be religious to be moral. Without God there is nothing to keep you from falling headlong into an abyss of moral relativism.

It is argued that without God as the Enforcer of an absolute moral standard - with the threat of hell and promise of heaven to back it up - people would engage in all sorts of unethical behaviors. I have always thought that this argument reveals more about the moral proclivity of the person making the argument than the morality of nonreligious people.

The need for morality is one of the arguments I have heard most often in favor of church attendance. Parents have told me that they bring their children to Sunday School to instill moral values in them. There is the belief that without religion morality has no foundation - at least no objective ethical foundation.

Unfortunately there is no evidence to support such a claim. Religious people do not have a monopoly on morality. Studies do not back up the claim that unless people are religious they would abandon themselves to immorality. Indeed some of the least religious countries – Sweden and Denmark for example – have the lowest rates of violent crime. The crime rate in the United States has been decreasing in the last decade, while at the same time belief in God and attendance at church has also been declining. That does not speak well for the influence of religion on social ethics.

A study measuring religious bodies in the United States, called the "2010 U.S. Religious Census: Religious Congregations & Membership Study," was commissioned by the Association of Statisticians of American Religious Bodies. It revealed that there is no correlation between the number of religious people in a city and the crime rate in that city. In fact some very religious cities were near the top of the list for assault, rape and property crime. State teen pregnancy rates and divorce rates were actually higher in states with higher religious participation.[56]

Atheists jump on such statistics and claim that religion makes one less moral! Not so fast! A study by Pennsylvania State University analyzed crime and religion data from 182 counties in three states. It showed that violent crime decreased as greater numbers of people were religiously active in a community. The effect was particularly pronounced in black violence within disadvantaged communities that are most likely to have the highest number of victims.

A Baylor University study of more than 15,000 people, ages 18 to 28, found that young adults who considered themselves religious were less likely than others to commit violent or property crimes. Those who claimed to be spiritual but set apart from organized religion were more likely to engage in both types of criminal activity.[57]

The majority of studies show no significant correlation between religiousness and morality. My examination of statistics of countries' crime rates and religiousness shows no clear correlation. In my opinion neither side of this debate has sufficient evidence to take the moral high ground and make the claim that religion – or lack of it – is any indication of morality.

Churches and pastors give the impression that Christianity has a clear set of morals securely moored in the Bible. But a cursory examination of the variety of moral convictions held by Christians on almost any issue reveals no consensus on what that standard of morality may be. Take the high profile moral issues – abortion, homosexuality, capital punishment, etc. Christians will disagree, and they all point to their Bible as their authority.

What your pastor won't tell you is that the Bible gives little moral guidance for any of the important ethical issues facing Christians today. Christian morality is a matter of how one interprets the Bible, and interpretations vary greatly. The moral imperatives that we take from Scripture depend on the moral convictions we bring to Scripture. A Quaker can find justification for pacifism and a Baptist for war. Let's look at the few areas that have been historically important for American Christians.

NATIONALISM

In the United States, God and country go together like mom and apple pie. Officially the law of the land is the separation of church and state, but in reality they are closely linked in the hearts and minds of American Christians. We display American flags in our church sanctuaries, much to the chagrin of foreign Christians visiting from other lands. We sing patriotic hymns in our churches on Memorial Day and the Fourth of July. We honor veterans during worship on Veterans Day. We pledge allegiance to the flag in Vacation Bible School and in private Christian schools. To be an American is to be a flag-waving, national anthem singing, Pledge of Allegiance reciting Christian.

In the above-mentioned service at the National Cathedral commemorating the victims of the 9/11 terrorist attacks, evangelist Billy Graham, who was known for anti-communism in his early days, espoused an idea that comes very close to the Islamic concept of shahid, the belief that those who die in holy war are guaranteed a place in paradise.

Without any knowledge of the victims' religious convictions, Graham made the extraordinary claim that many of those Americans who died in the twin towers went immediately to heaven. Graham's statement sounds very much like the beliefs of the jihadis, who flew the planes into the towers; they believed that their heroic self-sacrifice earned them a place in paradise.

Graham was verbalizing a long standing tenet of American Protestantism - that it is a sacred act to lay down your life for your country, especially in battle. Often the words of Jesus are quoted in this regard: "Greater love has no man than this, that a man lay down his life for his friends." (John 15:13) And by "friends" we mean "country."

I personally happen to agree with this type of patriotism. I love singing patriotic hymns in church. As a pastor I publicly honored those who served in the military in the worship service. I gladly preached and prayed at public Memorial Day services, and I still do. But I am not so hypocritical as to think I can find justification for any of this in the teachings of Jesus or elsewhere in the New Testament.

Our country was birthed in the American Revolution, whose justification for rebellion against the crown was "taxation without representation." In the name of "the Laws of Nature and of Nature's God" American colonists took up arms against their king because they believed they were being mistreated. But what did Jesus and the apostle Paul teach about paying taxes and taking up arms against the government?

Both Jesus and Paul made it clear that one was to pay taxes - without exceptions. When asked whether one should pay taxes to Caesar, Jesus said, "Render unto Caesar the things that are Caesar's, and unto God the things that are God's." (Mark 12:17) The apostle Paul goes further. He not only makes it clear that we are to pay taxes to the governing authorities, but that to do so is the will of God. Paul based his command to pay taxes on the premise that government is established by God.

Let every person be subject to the governing authorities. For there is no authority except from God, and those that exist have been instituted by God. Therefore whoever resists the authorities resists what God has appointed, and those who resist will incur judgment. For rulers are not a terror to good conduct, but to bad. Would you have no fear of the one who is in authority? Then do what is good, and you will receive his approval, for he is God's servant for your good. But if you do wrong, be afraid, for he does not bear the sword in vain. For he is the servant of God, an avenger who carries out God's wrath on the wrongdoer. Therefore one must be in subjection, not only to avoid God's wrath but also for the sake of conscience. For because of this you also pay taxes, for the authorities are ministers of God, attending to this very thing. Pay to all what is owed to them: taxes to whom taxes are owed, revenue to whom revenue is owed, respect to whom respect is owed, honor to whom honor is owed. (Romans 13:1-7)

The New Testament book of First Peter continues this theme. "Be subject for the Lord's sake to every human institution, whether it be to the emperor as supreme, or to governors as sent by him to punish those who do evil and to praise those who do good. For this is the will of God, that by doing good you should put to silence the ignorance of foolish people. Live as people who are free, not using your freedom as a cover-up for evil, but living as servants of God. Honor everyone. Love the brotherhood. Fear God. Honor the emperor." (I Peter 2:13-17)

Then there is Jesus' radical teaching on nonviolence, which conflicts with the idea of taking up arms. "You have heard that it was said, 'An eye for an eye and a tooth for a tooth.' But I say to you, Do not resist the one who is evil. But if anyone slaps you on the right cheek, turn to him the other also. And if anyone would sue you and take your tunic, let him have your cloak as well. And if anyone forces you to go one mile, go with him two miles. Give to the one who begs from you, and do not refuse the one who would borrow from you. You have heard that it was said, 'You shall love your neighbor and hate your enemy.' But I say to you, Love your enemies and pray for those who persecute you, so that you may be sons of your Father who is in heaven." (Matthew 5:38-45)

In that passage Jesus was referring to the practice of Roman soldiers in occupied Palestine requiring any Jew to carry his pack. I wonder what the American Founding Fathers would have said. When Jesus was being unfairly arrested for treason and blasphemy, he told his followers, "Put your sword back into its place. For all who take the sword will perish by the sword." (Matthew 26:52) According to the Gospel of John Jesus explained his rationale to the Roman governor Pilate, saying, "My kingdom is not of this world. If my kingdom were of this world, my servants would fight, that I might not be delivered over to the Jews. But my kingdom is not from the world." (John 18:36)

Christians search the teachings of Jesus or the New Testament in vain for any justification for armed rebellion against the government or nonpayment of taxes. Likewise one cannot find any justification for any type of armed resistance, not even in even self-defense. (One can find lots of support in the Old Testament, but not the New Testament.)

Christianity began as a religion of nonviolence. For three hundred years Christians would rather die a martyr's death than pick up a sword. That continued until the church gained earthly power; then it used the sword willingly to advance Church and state. As the saying goes, "Power corrupts and absolute power corrupts absolutely."

The Quakers and Mennonites have faithfully carried on the New Testament teaching and practice of nonviolence. Martin Luther King Jr and Mahatma Gandhi are much more in line with the teachings of Jesus than evangelical Christians and mainline Protestants. But it is not likely that your pastor will tell you that. He would not be so foolish as to encourage you to follow Jesus' ethic of nonviolence. It is much too controversial.

Churches have a hard enough time maintaining their membership without appearing unpatriotic. Look at the popular response to professional athletes "taking a knee" during the national anthem. This innocuous nonviolent protest is condemned as unpatriotic. Look at the rhetoric surrounding the "gun control" debate. Trying to pass legislation to protect schoolchildren from mass shooters is likened to treason. Americans love their guns and their country! Can you imagine what would happen if your pastor preached that Jesus required Christians to lay down their arms? Your pastor is not suicidal. That is why he won't tell you what Jesus really taught.

SLAVERY

The costliest war ever fought by the United States was the War Between the States. More American soldiers died in the American Civil War (almost 500,000) than in any other war we have fought. The major ethical issue of that war was slavery.

Today Americans are agreed in their condemnation of slavery, but in the 19th century the issue was hotly debated, even among Christians. Christians who sought guidance from God's Word concerning the morality of slavery found it difficult to condemn it on Biblical grounds. In fact the Bible never condemns, and often implicitly supports, the practice of slavery. That is something your pastor probably never told you.

Still many Christians took a stand against slavery. The abolitionist movement was begun by Quakers in the 18th century, both in England and America. The legal abolition of slavery was championed by 19th century abolitionists William Wilberforce and John Newton, who drew their convictions from their Christian faith. Harriet Beecher Stowe said that her influential book *Uncle Tom's Cabin* was inspired by a vision of a dying slave that she received during a communion service at the Bowdoin College chapel.

Christian denominations disagreed among themselves over the issue. Three of the nation's largest Protestant denominations — Presbyterians, Methodists, and Baptists — split over the issue of slavery. Baptists remained permanently divided, forming the Northern Baptist Convention (now American Baptists) and the Southern Baptist Convention.

Presbyterians were also of two minds. "As early as 1818, Presbyterians unanimously declared at their General Assembly that 'the voluntary enslaving of one part of the human race by another' is 'utterly inconsistent with the law of God.' Ironically, however, the same assembly upheld the decision to depose a Presbyterian minister because he held anti-slavery views. And in 1845, the General Assembly agreed that slavery was a biblical institution."[58]

The institution of slavery was supported by many Christians, especially Southern slaveholders, virtually all of whom would have identified themselves as Christians. In fact some argued that slavery was God's plan to evangelize the African "heathens." They quoted the Bible in support of their pro-slavery position.

The institution of slavery is mentioned throughout the Bible, yet it is never condemned. It is viewed as a normal part of society. Abraham, the patriarch of Judaism, Christianity, and Islam – as well as all the other biblical patriarchs - held slaves (Gen. 21:9–10). Canaan, Ham's son, was made a slave to his brothers by the decree of Noah, who according to the story "was a righteous man. He was blameless among the people of his time." (Genesis 6:9; 9:24–27). Indeed the enslavement of Ham's son Canaan was widely interpreted as referring to Africans, since Ham was considered to be black.

While prohibiting other practices, the Ten Commandments mention slavery twice in passing, but never condemns it, thereby showing God's implicit acceptance of it. (Ex. 20:10, 17). In the chapter following the Ten Commandments, there are numerous verses regulating slavery. In one of them it says that a man can beat his slave to death and not be punished for it, as long as it takes a day or two for the slave to die. If he dies immediately after the beating, then an undesignated punishment is applied. The explanation is "for he is his property." (Exodus 21:20-21)

If a man's ox gored a Hebrew man or woman to death, there were serious consequences. This included the death of the owner of the ox, if he knew that the ox was dangerous. But if the ox gored and killed a slave, the owner of the ox was to pay the slave's owner thirty shekels of silver. (Exodus 21:28-32) This clearly indicates that the humanity of the slave is in question.

Slavery was a common part of the Roman empire in which Jesus lived, yet he never condemned it. The apostle Paul exhorted slaves to obey their masters as if their owners were Christ himself. "Slaves, be obedient to those who are your masters according to the flesh, with fear and trembling, in the sincerity of your heart, as to Christ; not by way of eyeservice, as men-pleasers, but as slaves of Christ, doing the will of God from the heart. With good will render service, as to the Lord, and not to men, knowing that whatever good thing each one does, this he will receive back from the Lord, whether slave or free." (Ephesians 6:5–8 NASB).

When given the opportunity to help Onesimus, a fellow Christian and runaway slave, gain his freedom, Paul instead sent him back to his owner. He writes to the slaveholder: "I have sent him back to you in person, that is, sending my very heart, whom I wished to keep with me, so that on your behalf he might minister to me in my imprisonment for the gospel; but without your consent I did not want to do anything, so that your goodness would not be, in effect, by compulsion but of your own free will. For perhaps he was for this reason separated from you for a while, that you would have him back forever, no longer as a slave, but more than a slave, a beloved brother, especially to me, but how much more to you, both in the flesh and in the Lord." (Philemon 12-16)

In defense of Paul, he did speak on Onesimus' behalf, asking that his owner be lenient with him. But he never explicitly asks Philemon to free him. Although that is one possible interpretation of the phrase Paul uses when he says that he hopes Philemon would receive him as "no longer a slave but more than a slave, a beloved brother."

Over all Paul is more concerned that Philemon not feel like he had to do anything "by compulsion." But he is not concerned that Onesimus might have to live the rest of his life "by compulsion" as Philemon's property. The wishes of the slave Onesimus are not even considered in this little letter. I wonder how many Christian pastors would use this same Biblical reasoning and return a modern victim of the sex trafficking business to her owner. I suspect not many.

Slavery was such a part of Paul's Roman worldview that he uses the term as a synonym for being a follower of Christ. Paul often referred to himself as a "slave of Christ," thereby bestowing legitimacy on the term. It would be like Christians today using the N-word and calling themselves Christ's "n****r." The offensiveness of the term "slave" is obfuscated in modern translations, which substitute less controversial translations for the Greek word for slave (doulos), such as bondservant or simply servant. Modern readers could be excused for thinking that Paul thought of himself more like an English butler or footman – with holidays and Sundays off - than a piece of property.

There are some verses in the New Testament that were used to combat slavery, but they are few and far between. These were not explicit commands against slavery but themes or principles that needed to be applied. For example the Hebrews' liberation from slavery in Egypt provided fertile ground for African American preaching. Martin Luther King Jr used the imagery widely in his battle for civil rights. But one has to use such passages while being aware that Hebrews kept slaves even after they were freed from slavery.

The Apostle Paul wrote, "There is neither Jew nor Greek, there is neither slave nor free man, there is neither male nor female; for you are all one in Christ Jesus." (Galatians 3:28) Those are powerful words, which would in time be used against slavery, racism, and sexism. But at the time the apostle wrote these words, they were limited to one's standing before God, not one's standing in human society. These words were not quoted to abolish slavery until 1800 years later, when people with the belief in the equality of all human beings appropriated the verse for the cause of abolitionism.

History clearly shows that Christians did not find the clear moral guidance that they needed from Scripture when it came to this issue. Furthermore the issue of slavery is intimately connected to the issue of racism, especially in the United States. Today's American racism stems from the American heritage of the enslavement of Africans. To that sensitive and timely topic I will now turn.

RACISM

There is no such thing as race. It is a lie that has given rise to the sin of racism. There used to be different human races when there were various species of the genus Homo living on the face of the earth (i.e. Homo habilis, Homo erectus, etc.) But it has been 350,000 years since our closest cousins, Homo neanderthals, went extinct. Now there is only one race: the human race - Homo sapiens. Differences of skin color, hair texture, and eye shape are trivial variations in the genetic composition of humans, who originate from different geographical areas.

Yet "race" (better termed "ethnic origin") has been a big divider among humans, and racism is a serious problem even today. We need only turn on the television evening news to witness the effects of racism on American society. This is an issue that religion seems well-designed to address, because most modern religions allow people of different races to convert and be accepted as part of the group. Even Mormonism, which originated as a very racist religion, received a new revelation in 1978 that allowed people of dark skin to enter the Mormon priesthood.

Christianity – at least orthodox Christianity – likewise received a new revelation through the apostle Paul that allowed Gentiles into the family of God, previously reserved only for Israel. I quoted the key verse above. "There is neither Jew nor Greek, there is neither slave nor free man, there is neither male nor female; for you are all one in Christ Jesus." (Galatians 3:28) The Acts of the Apostles records how the inclusion of Gentiles – non-Jews – into the promises of God to the Jews came about.

Consequently the New Testament redefined the ethnic terms "Jew" and "Israel" to include those of all nations, not just those who carry the genes of Abraham and Jacob. The apostle Paul spends three chapters in his Letter to the Romans arguing for a new understanding of what it means to be the offspring of Abraham. "For he is not a Jew who is one outwardly, nor is circumcision that which is outward in the flesh. But he is a Jew who is one inwardly; and circumcision is that which is of the heart, by the

Spirit, not by the letter; and his praise is not from men, but from God." (Romans 2:28. See also Romans 3:29-30; 4:16-17 and Galatians 3:7-9)

When Christianity went from being a Jewish sect to becoming inclusive of every "nation" ("ethnos," meaning ethnic group), it transcended the category of race. Therefore one would think that Christianity would be the least racist religion in the world. But in America Sunday morning remains the most segregated time of the week.

In spite of some verses that teach racial equality and inclusivism, there are a lot of other verses in the Bible that teach racism. The Biblical roots of racism run deep. In the last section we saw how Southern Christians easily used the Bible to defend slavery. In the same way American Christians have used the Bible to defend segregation and racism. We saw in the section on Church History how anti-Semitism is deeply rooted in the New Testament. Anti-Semitism is just another form of racism.

Racism is also present in the Old Testament in the form of Semitism. Its basic premise is that one ethnic group has been elevated above all others by God. That is racism, no matter who the group is. In the Old Testament it is expressed in the idea that Israel alone is God's chosen people. Semitism (and its cousin Zionism) is just as racist as anti-Semitism. In practice it singles out those of Jewish descent for preferential treatment.

Unfortunately this form of primitive tribalism is growing in the modern state of Israel. In July 2018 the Israeli Knesset passed a controversial law declaring Israel to be officially "the Nation State of the Jewish People," effectively relegating Israeli-Arabs to the status of second class citizens.

In the debate leading up to that vote, Bradley Burston wrote in the Israeli newspaper *Haaretz* (April 4, 2018), "It hurts me to write what I'm about to. But it also hurts me to have to live in this place today... This is Zionism as racism. This is Israel at 70.... As a public servant, as an Orthodox rabbi, as a settler, you're free to say anything you want, as long as it's anti-Arab, anti-black, anti-Muslim, anti-Palestinian, anti-immigrant, and, for good measure, anti-Ashkenazi, anti-North American Jew, anti-New Israel Fund...."[59]

Allan Brownfeld writes in the June-July 2018 issue of *Washington Report on Middle East Affairs:*

Even a brief look at the growing racism and intolerance shows the direction in which contemporary Israel is headed. In March, for example, during his weekly sermon to the nation, Israel's Sephardic chief rabbi called black people "monkeys." Rabbi Yitzhak Yosef mentioned a blessing uttered upon seeing an "unusual creature," citing the example of a black person who has two white parents on the street in America. According to Ynet, Yosef referred to black people by the derogatory Hebrew word "kushi," and then went on to call a black person a "monkey." Yosef's fellow chief rabbi, Yisrael Lau, had already used this term to describe black people — on his very first day in office.

Dov Lior, chief rabbi of Hebron and Kiryat Arba and head of the "Council of Rabbis of Judea and Samaria," issued a religious edict saying "a thousand non-Jewish lives are not worth a Jew's fingernail." He said that Arabs arrested for terrorism could be used for medical experiments, and ruled that Jewish law forbids employing Arabs or renting homes to them. Ovadia Yosef, a deceased former Sephardi chief rabbi, said that the sole purpose of non-Jews "is to serve Jews." This declaration was later endorsed by some 250 other Jewish religious figures.[60]

This type of racism is rooted in the Bible. To be fair, the ancient Hebrew religion is not alone in holding racist origin myths. The idea is widespread. Countless primitive peoples saw themselves as "human beings" and other peoples as somehow less than fully human. Every people saw themselves as the favorites of their national gods. It just so happened that the ancient Hebrews' ethnocentrism became enshrined in a collection of sacred writings that became the scriptures for Judaism, Christianity, and (to a lesser extent) Islam.

Lest I be accused of anti-Semitism for equating the doctrine of Israel's election with racism, I need to confess that Christians have committed the same sin. Christians have claimed the same exalted status for ourselves, and we are equally wrong. Whereas Christianity expanded the idea of God's election to include those "from every nation, from all tribes and peoples and languages" (Revelation 7:9), Christians went on to develop their own form of spiritual exclusivism, based not on race but on religion.

Christians became the new chosen people, set apart from people of all other religions. "But you are a chosen race, a royal priesthood, a holy nation, a people for his own possession, that you may proclaim the excellencies of him who called you out of darkness into his marvelous light. Once you were not a people, but now you are God's people." (I Peter 2:9-10)

In this new dispensation Christians see themselves as the sole beneficiaries of God's grace. They are the only ones who will make it to heaven. Only those who believe in Jesus will be saved. People of all other faiths are eternally lost. The one unforgiveable sin is not believing in Jesus. Christ is reported to have said in the Gospel of John, which is also the most anti-Semitic gospel in the canon, "The world's sin is that it refuses to believe in me." (John 16:9)

According to orthodox Christian theology, if you are not a Christian, your eternal destiny is "outer darkness where there is weeping a gnashing of teeth," (Matthew 25:30) also described as a "blazing furnace" (Matthew 13:50) where non-Christians suffer "the punishment of eternal fire." (Jude 1:7) It is no surprise that it was Germany, the homeland of the Protestant Reformation, which conceived of the Third Reich, a millennial reign for the chosen Aryan race, and concentration camps for others. Nazi extermination camps were earthly replicas of the Christian hell, complete with burning ovens.

The Hebrew prophets saw the danger of this idea of a "chosen people" and preached against the racism inherent in the concept. The 7th century BC Deuteronomist recorded how God tried to remove Israel from their pedestal of self-aggrandizement. He wrote, "It was not because you were more in number than any other people that the Lord set his love on you and chose you, for you were the fewest of all peoples, but it is because the Lord loves you and is keeping the oath that he swore to your fathers, that the Lord has brought you out with a mighty hand and redeemed you from the house of slavery, from the hand of Pharaoh king of Egypt." (Deuteronomy 7:7-8)

The eighth century BC prophet Amos put Israel's election in perspective when he prophesied these words of the Lord God of Hosts: "'Are not you Israelites the same to me as the Cushites?' declares the Lord. 'Did I not bring Israel up from Egypt, the Philistines from Caphtor and the Arameans from Kir?'" (Amos 9:7 NIV) Did you hear that? God said that the Israelites were the same to him as other peoples! They were not any more "chosen" than the Cushites, Philistines and Arameans.

The Cushites were Africans inhabiting what is now Ethiopia, Sudan and Eritrea. The Arameans are the Syrians. And the Philistines ... well, they were a sea-faring people who settled on the coast of Canaan. We get the word Palestine from them. Palestinians are their descendants.

Amos is saying that East Africans, Palestinians, and Syrians were also chosen by God, delivered from bondage in a foreign country, and presumably brought to their own promised lands. The land of the biblical Philistines is the present-day Gaza Strip. According to God's Word the Palestinians are as much God's chosen people as the Jews, and they were in the land of Canaan before the Hebrews!

Speaking of the Land of Canaan, we have to address the issue of racial genocide in the Bible. The racism found in the West can be traced in no small part to racism in the Bible. In the Old Testament God orders the destruction of whole groups of people. Today we call it ethnic cleansing. He ordered the mass slaughter of all the indigenous peoples of Canaan in order to make room for his chosen people Israel. The Book of Deuteronomy says:

"When the LORD your God brings you into the land you are entering to possess and drives out before you many nations—the Hittites, Girgashites, Amorites, Canaanites, Perizzites, Hivites and Jebusites, seven nations larger and stronger than you — and when the LORD your God has delivered them over to you and you have defeated them, then you must destroy them totally. Make no treaty with them, and show them no mercy. Do not intermarry with them. Do not give your daughters to their sons or take their daughters for your sons". (Deut.7:1-3 NIV)

It does not stretch our imagination to imagine how Americans raised on the Bible might have patterned their treatment of the indigenous peoples of North America on Israel's treatment of the indigenous peoples of Canaan. Like Israel America saw itself as a chosen people fulfilling their manifest destiny of occupying America from sea to shining sea. What better model to use to accomplish this divinely appointed plan than the Word of God?

The story of the Amalekites is particularly revealing. The Amalekites were one branch of the descendants of Edom (Esau, Jacob's brother) from whom the people of Jordan today are said to be descended. When God chose the first king of Israel, he gave him a command through the prophet Samuel. "And Samuel said to Saul, "The Lord sent me to anoint you king over his people Israel; now therefore listen to the words of the Lord. Thus says the Lord of hosts, 'I have noted what Amalek did to Israel in opposing them on the way when they came up out of Egypt. Now go and strike Amalek and devote to destruction all that they have. Do not spare them, but kill both man and woman, child and infant, ox and sheep, camel and donkey.'" (I Samuel 15:1-3)

When Saul failed to fulfill this command completely, it was grounds for God to disown him and choose another man as king. This man was David, "a man after God's own heart." (1 Samuel 13:14; Acts 13:22) Saul's reluctance to exterminate every single Amalekite is the reason why Israel was placed in danger centuries later by an Amalekite named Haman, who sought to exterminate the Jews, just as they had tried to do to his people. It took Queen Esther to finish the job that Saul had started. This is no minor story. This Jewish slaughter of their enemies recorded in the Old Testament book of

Esther is celebrated annually today in the Jewish festival of Purim.

The belief that Israel is God's chosen people is not a harmless bit of ancient theology. It motivates people today. It has led modern day Israel to claim the land of Israel for itself and to occupy land on the West Bank as a divine right. The Bible is considered to be Israel's deed to the Holy Land, as Israel's legendary Foreign Minister Abba Eban declared from the podium of the United Nations general assembly, while holding a Bible in his hand. This claim was repeated as recently as 2015 by Knesset Speaker Yuli Edelstein.[61] "The Land of Israel belongs to the People of Israel" is the longstanding slogan of Religious Zionism.

It has led modern evangelical Christians to defend the right of Israel to take Palestinian land by force and kill Palestinian people if they resist. It is sad to see American Christians, who should be championing the democratic rights of all people, especially Palestinian Christians, being sucked into an ancient form of racism – all in the name of the Jesus Christ.

When Christians today look to the New Testament for help in addressing racism we are faced with a troubling Biblical witness. On the one hand there are powerful passages that can be used to speak against racism, mostly in the Book of Acts and the Letters of

Paul. On the other hand there are passages that stereotype ethnic groups, such as this: "One of the Cretans, a prophet of their own, said, 'Cretans are always liars, evil beasts, lazy gluttons.' This testimony is true." (Titus 1:12) That is the definition of racism.

Racism is alive and well in American Christianity. But it is a sin. God does not play favorites. We are all God's people. Neither Jews nor Christians have a monopoly on God's love, grace, truth ... or Middle Eastern real estate. This is likely something your pastor has never told you.

HOMOSEXUALITY

Every generation of Christians has a defining issue that divides it. Today it is homosexuality. The right of gay, lesbian, and transgender persons to full inclusion in American society and in the Christian church divides churches and denominations. Every major Protestant denomination is having to confront the issue. I have had to deal with it throughout my ministry. From the time I first entered fulltime Christian ministry in the late 1970's I have had gay and lesbian church members. More often than not, they were leaders in my congregations.

One of my best friends (my roommate during college and after college, a groomsman in my wedding, and later an ordained Unitarian

Universalist minister) was gay. He agonized over his sexual orientation for years. He eventually took his own life because the struggle was more than he could bear. To this day I wonder if there was something I could have said or done to prevent the untimely death of my dear friend.

The Baptist church that I served in western Pennsylvania for eleven years left the American Baptist denomination over the issue. I often wonder if I could have handled that situation differently. In hindsight I think I could have navigated those rough waters better than I did. I regret that I did not guide that congregation better in its decision-making process.

The church I served most recently in New Hampshire (of which I am still a member, but no longer its pastor) is associated with both American Baptists and United Methodists. They took a vote this summer (2018) to permit same sex weddings in their buildings. This puts them in violation of the United Methodist *Book of Discipline*, which prohibits Methodist clergy from conducting such weddings and prohibits Methodist church buildings to be used for such weddings. It also contradicts the stated policy of American Baptists, which says that "the practice of homosexuality is incompatible with Biblical teaching."

In both of these church cases, the issue strained relations within the congregation and with the denomination. Though each congregation decided the issue very differently, in both cases people left the church. It is a contentious subject which divides Christians, congregations and denominations. People on both sides feel very strongly about the issue, and both feel like they are on the side of God.

When one looks to the Scriptures for guidance on this issue, it appears at first glance that conservatives have the winning hand. There are many passages that condemn homosexuality in the strongest terms. These verses are the banners under which conservatives lead their crusade against "sexuality immorality" and the decline of moral values in America.

But when one looks carefully at the context of these polemical verses, it becomes clear that the issue is not as simple as it first appears. In the Old Testament the prohibition of homosexual acts is found in the laws of Leviticus and Deuteronomy.

Leviticus says, "You shall not lie with a male as with a woman. It is an abomination." (18:22) "If a man lies with a male as he lies with a woman, both of them have committed an abomination." (Lev. 20:13) Deuteronomy 22:5 extends the prohibition to clothing, apparently addressing the transgender issue. "A woman shall not wear anything that pertains to a man, nor shall a man put on a woman's garment, for all who do so are an abomination to the LORD your God."

You can't get any clearer than that, right? But when one looks at the context of these verses, cracks appear in the conservative's case. The verses immediately before Leviticus 18:22 prohibit intercourse during menstruation (18:19) and adultery (18:20), putting them in the same category as child sacrifice (18:21) and bestiality (18:23). These are all part of the same Holiness Code of Leviticus, chapters 17-26.

If we move ahead a few verses in Leviticus 18 we find prohibitions against interbreeding cattle, hybrid crops, and clothing made of blended fabrics. "You shall not let your cattle breed with a different kind. You shall not sow your field with two kinds of seed, nor shall you wear a garment of cloth made of two kinds of material." (Lev. 19:19) Then there are the prohibitions against beard trimming and tattoos (Lev. 19:27-28). Yet I don't hear anyone calling for boycotts of local grocery stores, clothing shops, barbers and tattoo parlors.

In interpreting these passages in the Old Testament one cannot single out homosexual acts for special treatment and ignore the surrounding verses. If we can declare that today it is not a sin to cut your beard, get a tattoo, breed cattle, grow hybrid vegetables, or wear a wool-cotton sweater, then why can't we say it is not a sin to be in a committed homosexual relationship?

When one looks to the New Testament, one notices that homosexuality is never mentioned by Jesus. On the other hand other forms of sexual behavior are proscribed. Adultery is addressed directly by Jesus, as is divorce. Jesus said, "Anyone who divorces his wife and marries another woman commits adultery, and the man who marries a divorced woman commits adultery." (Luke 16:18)

It is hypocritical for a pastor to take a moral stand against gay marriage (never mentioned by Jesus) while regularly conducting weddings of divorced persons (a practice condemned by Jesus). If we can believe that the remarriage of divorced persons is not sin, why can't we say that gay marriage is not sin? To single out homosexuality for special condemnation is the definition of hypocrisy and homophobia.

Another Biblical reference often quoted is the sin of Sodom and Gomorrah. After all, homosexual intercourse is called sodomy! The identification of the sin of Sodom with homosexuality is based on the story of Lot and his daughters in Genesis 19.

Lot had given some angels (disguised as men) lodging for the night in his home in Sodom. A mob gathered outside his house demanding to have sex with the visitors. Lot refuses, but offers his daughters to the mob instead. (Not a good example of superior morality!) The angels strike the mob with blindness, and Lot's family escapes the city just before it is destroyed by God with fire and brimstone.

The sin of Sodom was homosexuality, right? The New Testament book of Jude seems to concur. "Sodom and Gomorrah and the surrounding cities, which likewise indulged in sexual immorality and pursued unnatural desire, serve as an example by undergoing a punishment of eternal fire." (Jude 1:7) But upon closer inspection it seems more likely that this verse is referring to angel-human union, since the first half of that sentence refers to angels who "left their proper dwelling," apparently to come to earth. This is likely a reference to the story of angel-human interbreeding in Genesis 6:1-4.

There is more to the story of Sodom according to the prophet Ezekiel. After calling Jerusalem an adulterous wife and a prostitute, God says: "As I live, declares the Lord God, your sister Sodom and her daughters have not done as you and your daughters have done. Behold, this was the guilt of your sister Sodom: she and her daughters had pride, excess of food, and prosperous ease, but did not aid the poor and needy. They were haughty and did an abomination before me. So I removed them, when I saw it." (Ezekiel 16:48-50)

It appears that the sin of Sodom was actually "pride, excess of food, and prosperous ease" and "not aiding the poor and needy." Yet I suspect that we will not hear evangelical and conservative preachers condemn these as forms of "sodomy." In fact many churches condone such sins when they preach their Prosperity Gospel and eat their potluck suppers. Why? Because they coincide with their church culture and conservative political agenda.

Most of the New Testament's condemnation of homosexuality comes from the Pauline epistles. The apostle Paul writes, "Do you not know that the unrighteous will not inherit the kingdom of God? Do not be deceived. Neither fornicators, nor idolaters, nor adulterers, nor homosexuals, nor sodomites, nor thieves, nor covetous, nor drunkards, nor revilers, nor extortioners will inherit the kingdom of God." (I Corinthians 6:9-10)

The Pastoral Epistles of First and Second Timothy include similar passages:

"But we know that the law is good if one uses it lawfully, knowing this: that the law is not made for a righteous person, but for the lawless and insubordinate, for the ungodly and for sinners, for the unholy and profane, for murderers of fathers and murderers of mothers, for manslayers, for fornicators, for sodomites, for kidnappers, for liars, for perjurers, and if there is any other thing that is contrary to sound doctrine, according to the glorious gospel of the blessed God which was committed to my trust. (I Timothy 1:8-11)

"But know this, that in the last days perilous times will come: For men will be lovers of themselves, lovers of money, boasters, proud, blasphemers, disobedient to parents, unthankful, unholy, unloving, unforgiving, slanderers, without self-control, brutal, despisers of good, traitors, headstrong, haughty, lovers of pleasure rather than lovers of God, 5 having a form of godliness but denying its power. And from such people turn away! (2 Timothy 3:1-5)

The lengthiest New Testament passage against homosexuality is Romans 1:18-32. After describing and condemning homosexual practices, Paul lumps them with a long list of sins. He says they are "all manner of unrighteousness, evil, covetousness, malice. They are full of envy, murder, strife, deceit, maliciousness. They are gossips, slanderers, haters of God, insolent, haughty, boastful, inventors of evil, disobedient to parents, foolish, faithless, heartless, ruthless. Though they know God's righteous decree that those who practice such things deserve to die, they not only do them but give approval to those who practice them." (1:29-32)

Note the context in which homosexuality is mentioned. It is part of a long list of sins. If one condemns the practice of homosexuality, then one must also condemn the other things mentioned. That would include alcoholism, covetousness, love of money, disobedience to parents, unthankfulness, unforgiveness, love of pleasure, self-love, etc.

To cherry-pick homosexuality for special condemnation is the epitome of hypocrisy. Indeed to do so would probably come under the headings of haughty, unloving, unforgiving, gossip, slander, heartless, which are listed equally as bad. If we single out the sexual behavior of gays, lesbians, and transgender persons for special scorn, then we better be prepared for God's judgment on our own hypocrisy, which is the sin Jesus often singles out for special condemnation. As Jesus is reported to have said to the crowd ready to stone the woman caught in adultery, "Let he who is without sin cast the first stone." (John 8:7)

When we look at what the Bible really says about homosexuality in context, we discover that the case against homosexual practice (and therefore related issues such as same sex marriage) is not as simple as we may have thought. Sexual orientation and gender identity are complex issues with biological, psychological, and sociological elements. It is not simply a matter of moral choice.

It is true that gays and lesbians were condemned as sinners in the New Testament. That cannot be denied. But the New Testament also condemns women who wear expensive clothing, jewelry and braided hair. "Do not let your adorning be external — the braiding of hair and the putting on of gold jewelry, or the clothing you wear." (1 Peter 3:3-4) "Women should adorn themselves in respectable apparel, with modesty and self-control, not with braided hair and gold or pearls or costly attire." (1 Timothy 2:9)

It is also true that Jesus associated with sinners. We are told that he hung out with prostitutes, tax collectors (extortioners), drunkards, and a host of other "sinners." And he was regularly criticized by the religious people of his day for doing so.

The gospels do not specifically mention homosexuals among Jesus' entourage. If they had been identified they would have been stoned on the spot, like the woman caught in adultery. But I think it likely that LGBTQ persons were among the first followers of Jesus. If Jesus accepted them as his brothers and sisters, shouldn't we? Jesus said, "Whatever you did to the least of these my brothers and sisters, you have done to me." (Matthew 25:40)

It was not long ago that "mixed marriages," meaning interracial marriages, were forbidden in many states of our country. But we know better now.

It is time for the church to "know better" about gay marriage.

Interreligious marriage is still banned in many conservative Jewish, Christian, and Muslim traditions. For Christians such a marriage is seen as being "unequally yoked." (2 Corinthians 6:14) But such religious values – especially of the majority religion - must not be imposed upon the wider community.

When it comes to the inclusion of LGBTQ persons in society, I believe that they should have the same standing as any other persons, including the right to marry and adopt children. To amend Paul's famous words of inclusion, "There is neither Jew nor Greek, neither slave nor free, neither male nor female, *neither straight nor gay*; for you are all one in Christ Jesus." Therefore I gladly welcome them into full membership in the life of the church.

It is not a sin to be attracted to a person of the same sex or to be in a committed relationship – including marriage - with someone of the same sex. It is sin to condemn people based on sexual orientation and gender identity. In my opinion it is a sin for Christians to refuse to sell wedding cakes, wedding flowers, or wedding invitations to gay couples.

The Christian church is not the sex police of American society. We are called to love all people

unconditionally with the love of our Lord Jesus
Christ. Then, as the song says, they will know we are
Christians by our love.

OTHER ISSUES

There are many other ethical issues facing the
church today. As I write this chapter a grand jury in
Pennsylvania just announced the most recent
installment of the Roman Catholic Church's sordid
tale of predator priests. This episode involves three
hundred priests abusing more than a thousand
children across Pennsylvania over seven decades, all
the while being covered up by the church hierarchy. If
there is any example that demonstrates that being
religious does not equate with morality, it is this.

On another issue Pope Francis recently announced
that his church is now officially opposed to the death
penalty, suddenly reversing centuries of moral
guidance on this momentous issue of life and death.
But I guess you could say, "Better late than never."

Our country is presently in the midst of the
#MeToo movement, exposing sexual assault across
virtually every segment of our society. This calls
attention to the deeper problem of sexism and
misogyny, not only in secular society but in the
Christian Church. Megachurch pastors are being

expelled regularly for inappropriate relationships with female employees and parishioners.

There is the related issue of abortion and reproductive rights that continues to divide the nation forty-five years after Roe v. Wade. Pro-Life advocates proclaim that God's Word clearly defends the sanctity of human life and the full humanity of the unborn. But one looks through the pages of scripture in vain for such clear statements.

Oft-quoted Psalm 139 declares that God knit us together in our mother's womb. But when we look at Old Testament passages that specifically address the death of unborn children, we see that the full humanity of the child is in question. For example in Exodus 21 (right after the Ten Commandments) it says that if a man strikes a woman and she miscarries, then there are consequences. If the child is lost, then the man is fined an amount determined by the husband. If the woman dies, then the principle of "lex talionis" kicks in - "a life for a life." The child appears to be considered less human than the mother. Of course there are alternative interpretations of this passage, as one would expect. But this is the scholarly consensus.

Then there is the issue of ageism, which is often linked with sexism. A revealing passage in Leviticus 27 puts a monetary value on people of different ages.

It reads: "The Lord spoke to Moses, saying, 'Speak to the people of Israel and say to them, If anyone makes a special vow to the Lord involving the valuation of persons, then the valuation of a male from twenty years old up to sixty years old shall be fifty shekels of silver, according to the shekel of the sanctuary. If the person is a female, the valuation shall be thirty shekels. If the person is from five years old up to twenty years old, the valuation shall be for a male twenty shekels, and for a female ten shekels. If the person is from a month old up to five years old, the valuation shall be for a male five shekels of silver, and for a female the valuation shall be three shekels of silver. And if the person is sixty years old or over, then the valuation for a male shall be fifteen shekels, and for a female ten shekels.'" (Leviticus 27:1-7) Males ages 20 to 60 are of full value. The rest of us, less so. Thus saith the Lord.

There is the issue of greed and covetousness, although people will not use those words. We use positive terms like wealth, success, and "the American dream," which are touted as virtues in our American culture. But the reality is that the never-ending consumerist lust for the newest and best material things is the foundation of capitalism and the free enterprise system.

Love of money is a sin in the Bible, but a virtue in our country. What Alexis de Tocqueville observed of

Americans in the nineteenth century is even truer today: "I know of no country where the love of money has taken stronger hold on the affections of men. Love of money is either the chief or secondary motive in everything Americans do."

But the Bible forbids coveting in the Ten Commandments, and the New Testament equates it with idolatry. (Colossians 3:5) 1 Timothy 6:10 says, "For the love of money is a root of all kinds of evils. It is through this craving that some have wandered away from the faith and pierced themselves with many pangs." Yet the wealthy are coddled in American churches as valued benefactors, in direct opposition to the teachings of Scripture. (James 2:1-7)

The charging of interest is integral to the American economic system, yet it is forbidden in scripture. Not only exorbitant rates of interest (as charged in payday loans) but charging any interest at all is called usury in the Bible and outlawed for the people of God. Yet it is never challenged by "Bible-believing" Christians in our American society.

There is no shortage of issues that I could address in this chapter. I could easily triple the number of topics addressed in this chapter, and I would still leave out ones that someone considers important. To address all worthy subjects would greatly extend the length of this book.

When one searches the pages of Scripture for divine direction on important modern issues, one is stymied by a lack of guidance. For example the historic relegation of women to the status of second class Christians in the church – and in professional Christian ministry in particular - is shameful. Yet one can find ample scripture texts forbidding leadership to women. The passages supporting female leadership are fewer and more nuanced. One often has to read between the lines. Yet all but the most conservative and fundamentalist churches have embraced women as clergy and lay leaders.

Sexual assault of women by men in positions of authority is rampant in the Bible. There is the story (mentioned earlier) of Lot, who is described by the New Testament book of Second Peter as "a righteous man, who was distressed by the depraved conduct of the lawless." (2 Peter 2:7) Yet in Genesis 19 this righteous man offers to give his two daughters to a mob of lawless men to rape, in order to protect two men who were staying in his house. To sweeten the offer, he points out to the rapists that his daughter are virgins.

In the Book of Judges there is a similar story of a man who offered his virgin daughter to a mob who wanted to rape a Levite who was a guest under his roof. When the mob refused, the Levite threw his concubine out the door, where the men raped her to death. (Judges 19) To make matters worse, the Levite then cuts her body into pieces and distributes the pieces to the twelve tribes of Israel as a testimony against the mob. There is no thought that he might have done something unethical by not protecting her.

Unfortunately these stories are not the exception. In an opinion piece in the *New York Times* entitled "The Bible's #MeToo Problem," Lutheran pastor Emily Scott relates how the Biblical stories of women like Dinah, Tamar, and Bathsheba read like modern examples of sexual assault. [62] The Bible has a #MeToo problem, which means that we who look to the Bible for moral guidance have a problem.

The similar issue of the abuse of children ought to be a no-brainer. How could anyone condone the killing or abuse of children? But in the Bible we have God ordering the killing of children, not only as part of holy war but in other cases. For example in 2 Kings 2:23-25 the prophet Elisha calls on the name of God to send a bear to maul (and apparently kill) a group of boys for making fun of his bald head. Then we have the perverse blessing of Psalm 137:9 "Blessed shall he be who takes your little ones and dashes them against the rock!" I bet your pastor has not preached on that verse recently.

In short when we look to the Bible to give us clear guidance on the pressing moral issues of our time we come up short. Instead of unambiguous pronouncements from God, we have a confusing collage of passages that support both sides of any given issue. The reason that Christians, churches, and denominations take different sides on moral issues is because different books in Scriptures have different views.

The Bible reflects the moral (and immoral) climate of the time it was written. Very seldom are the Bible writers able to transcend their cultural milieu to give us superior moral guidance relevant to today. It is always a matter of interpretation. One of the Ten Commandments says, "Thou shalt not kill." Does that apply to war, as the Quakers say, and Jesus seems to concur? Does it apply to national policies that result in poverty and starvation on the other side of the world? Does it apply to abortion? The death penalty? How about killing animals for sport ... or food?

The uncomfortable truth - that your pastor won't tell you - is that the Bible gives little guidance on how to address the important moral issues of our day. It is a matter of interpretation, and how we interpret a passage depends on the moral principles we bring to the text. As much as Christians profess to take our morality from the Bible, the reality is that we bring it to the Bible. We find our ethics in other places and use the Bible to garner proof texts for positions that we already hold. We do this to give our conclusions the divine imprimatur "Thus saith the Lord!"

.

7

WHAT YOU CAN DO TO HELP YOUR PASTOR

One thing your pastor won't tell you is that she needs your help. Being a pastor is hard work. That is something a lot of people – especially people in the church – do not understand. I am not saying that the ministry is more difficult than other jobs. I wouldn't know. Except for summer and part-time jobs during college and seminary, I have never done anything else. So I wouldn't know from personal experience if it is more difficult than other jobs. But the chances are you don't know what it is like to be a pastor either!

A lot of people have confided in me over the years how difficult their jobs are. In my congregations I have had prison guards, coal miners, farmers, police officers, soldiers, nurses, physicians, teachers, judges, lawyers, airline pilots, air traffic controllers, and members of many other professions. From what they have told me, their jobs can be very difficult. In most cases the pay does not make up for the emotional stress and long hours.

I don't know if my job is more difficult than theirs. My guess is that it is more difficult than some and less than others. But I do know that being a pastor is difficult. On more than one occasion I have come close to giving it up, only to change my mind. Over the years I have watched many of my friends leave ministry for other – less stressful and better paying - jobs and careers.

Early in my ministry I went to the Center for Career Development and Ministry, which at the time was on the campus of the Andover Newton Theological School. As part of a career assessment, a counselor told me, "You are good for the ministry, but the ministry is not good for you." The saying became a mantra, which my wife and I repeated during difficult times. In some ways the counselor was right and in other ways wrong. I am glad I remained in the ministry, but it wasn't easy.

One thing I have learned is that a pastor needs help – a lot of it. That is something your pastor won't tell you, but I will because I am retired. There is one thing he needs in particular. He needs you to be open. In this chapter I list some ways you can be open.

OPEN YOUR MIND

There is nothing more refreshing than entertaining new ideas. There is nothing sadder than a person who has all the answers. They cannot learn anything new. Keep an open mind about everything. Allow your deepest beliefs and convictions to be challenged.

Not long ago I wrote a book entitled *Thank God for Atheists: What Christians Can Learn from the New Atheism*. It was the product of years of reading – and listening with an open mind – to ideas that challenged my deepest beliefs and convictions. Even though it is not one of my best received books (which is no surprise since Christians are loath to think that atheists are right about anything), it is one of my personal favorites. Researching it forced me to think in new ways. It made me wrestle with God. It made me confront idols in my life. It transformed my theology in surprising ways. It made me a more careful thinker and (I hope) a better, although more unconventional, Christian.

Your pastor needs you to keep an open mind. Not so open that your brains fall out. Not so open-minded that you are "tossed back and forth by the waves, and blown here and there by every wind of teaching and by the cunning and craftiness of people in their deceitful scheming." (Ephesians 4:14 NIV)

But neither should our faith be so closed to new ideas that we have to check our brains at the door whenever we come into church. We should not be so closed-minded that we are blind and deaf to truth when it is placed before us.

Your pastor has a lot of new ideas that she learned in seminary, in continuing education courses, at conferences, and in her personal reading. Some of them you will not like. In fact *most* of them you will not like! But your pastor needs you to keep an open mind about them.

Some of the ideas might be ones that I have presented in this book. Ideas about what the Bible really teaches. She might preach some theological ideas that feel challenging to you. They might even feel (heaven forbid) unorthodox. Remember that even orthodox doctrines were once new ideas.

She might present scientific truths that challenge your theological beliefs. Keep an open mind and investigate them objectively for yourself. She might give a new perspective on church history, which may challenge the ways you think about Christianity.

She will almost certainly present new ideas about doing ministry. Different ways of worshipping. Different ways of reaching out to unusual types of peoples. Your pastor has some wonderful new ideas!

Take a chance on them, even if they are outside your comfort zone.

Make it a personal rule to initially say "Yes" to any new idea raised by your pastor. That doesn't mean that every idea she has is great. Some might be awful. But don't reject anything out of hand, no matter how uncomfortable it may make you feel. You can always say "No" later if the idea proves to be a dud. Trust the process. Trust that the Spirit will guide your church to "test the spirits to see if they are of God." (I John 4:1)

The chances are that your pastor has given a lot of thought and prayer to any new idea she presents. So give it a try. All you have to lose is the status quo. You have called her to lead the congregation. Let her lead! One thing for sure, if the American church keeps on going in the direction it is now, it will be as good as dead in a couple of generations. Best case scenario, it will be an irrelevant institution with empty pews and dwindling budgets, kept alive only by endowment funds. The church desperately needs fresh ideas – really new and different ideas. So keep an open mind.

Remain open to truth, wherever and however it appears. The spiritual life is a never-ending quest for greater understanding. Remember that all truth is God's truth, whether it is found in science, philosophy, or other religious traditions.

Truth is by nature iconoclastic. Truth smashes idols, wherever they are found. That includes ecclesiastical idols and theological idols, which are the most dangerous of all gods. Theology, especially when hardened into creeds and doctrinal statements, is the most insidious form of idolatry. It gives the appearance of spiritual truth, while serving as a barrier to experiencing spiritual truth. It presents the illusion of finality and certainty, while actually being an imperfect pointer to Truth.

Be unafraid to venture beyond familiar ground into uncharted territory, for that is where God is found. God appears in the wilderness, and not in the well-trampled temple courts, which are the domain of money-changers. Their tables must be overturned if the house of God is to be cleansed and true worship is to occur. Never be deceived into thinking that you have the truth. You will never possess truth. Truth possesses you. If you think you've got it, be assured you don't.

OPEN YOUR BIBLE

Christianity and the Bible have been intricately connected since the beginning. The Church gave birth to the Bible during those years when the early Christian documents were being written and canonized. In return the Bible gave birth to successive generations of Christians. Now that process is in danger of ending. Christianity has become unmoored from its scriptures. Today's Christians are Biblically illiterate. Regularly conducted surveys confirm that diagnosis.

According to the American Bible Society, 87 percent of American households own a Bible, and the average household has three. But people aren't reading their Bibles. I remember one woman in Pennsylvania who started attending our church and adult Sunday School class. She expressed interest in reading the Bible, but she didn't have one. So a generous member of my congregation presented her with a large study Bible as a gift. When I later went by her house to visit, I inquired about how she was enjoying her new Bible. She pointed to the Bible laying on the floor. She was using it as a doorstop! (At least she got some use out of it, rather than just letting it collect dust on a bookshelf.)

According to a 2017 Lifeway Survey more than half of Americans (53%) have read no more than a few passages or stories from the Bible in their lifetime. Whereas 20% report having read the whole Bible at least once, a higher percentage (23%) have never opened it or have read only a few sentences. [63] Comprehension and retention of the Bible's content is even worse.

Quoting recent Gallup and Barna data, Albert Mohler, president of the Southern Baptist Theological Seminary writes, "Fewer than half of all adults can name the four gospels. Many Christians cannot identify more than two or three of the disciples. According to data from the Barna Research Group, 60 percent of Americans can't name even five of the Ten Commandments.... According to 82 percent of Americans, 'God helps those who help themselves,' is a Bible verse.... A Barna poll indicated that at least 12 percent of adults believe that Joan of Arc was Noah's wife. Another survey of graduating high school seniors revealed that over 50 percent thought that Sodom and Gomorrah were husband and wife. A considerable number of respondents to one poll indicated that the Sermon on the Mount was preached by Billy Graham. We are in big trouble."[64]

Regardless of whether you are conservative or liberal – and whether your pastor is conservative or liberal – you would do your pastor a big favor if you opened your Bible. If you read it, it will surprise you. Barna's 2018 "State of the Bible" survey reports that more than half of those who read the Bible monthly report that it positively affected their spiritual growth.[65] On the other hand atheists report that reading the Bible caused them to become atheists!

Yuriy Stasyuk was an evangelical pastor who became an atheist and now blogs as "The Reluctant

Skeptic." He describes his own experience. "Reading the Bible is my personal reason for leaving the church. Close to a dozen people that I have talked with have also reported this as being the most important and influential factor in their journey. In my purely anecdotal experience, it seems that most of these people, including myself, were overly devout (many were or wanted to be preachers/pastors/etc). For us, it was reading the biblical texts with extreme reverence and dedication, especially those passages that people really tend to avoid, spurred our critical analysis of the religion we held very dear. In my own case, [it was] reading the Bible and noticing numerous contradictions, scientific errors, and morally reprehensible actions and commands that pulled the rug out from underneath me. I very reluctantly gave up my dearest friend, my faith, only when I exerted every attempt in apologetics to defend the things I was reading in the Bible. I simply could not dishonestly placate my emotions by fallacious apologetic arguments; I sincerely love truth, and would be willing to believe in anything, as long as there is good justification and evidence, but not without it, and especially not against it."[66]

As he mentions, he is not the only one who has had this experience. Isaac Asimov said, "Properly read, the Bible is the most potent force for atheism ever conceived." Mark Twain said, "It ain't those parts of the Bible that I can't understand that bother me, it is the parts that I do understand." It has become something of a meme in atheist circles today to say, "The quickest route to atheism is reading the Bible." It is a clever saying, but I have seen no data to back it up.

It is true that atheists and agnostics are more knowledgeable about religious beliefs than Christians. The 2010 *US Religious Knowledge Survey* by the Pew Research Center revealed that atheists and agnostics are the highest-scoring group on religious knowledge, outperforming evangelical Protestants, mainline Protestants and Catholics on questions about the Bible, religious teachings, history and leading figures of major world religions.[67] The average atheist knows more about the Bible than Christians do!

The Pew Research Center suspected that this may be because atheists and agnostics have higher levels of education, which would explain their performance on the religious knowledge survey. However, even after controlling for levels of education and other key demographic traits (race, age, gender and region), significant differences in religious knowledge persist among adherents of various faith traditions. Atheists and agnostics still have the highest levels of religious knowledge.[68]

The Pew survey raises another important matter. It is important that we not only read the Bible, but also read the Scriptures of other religions. It always amazes me how little Christians know about the beliefs and traditions of other faiths. But that does not stop Christians from being arrogant in their ignorance!

A few years ago I led a five-week study of the Tao Te Ching at a local yoga center. (That raised more than a few eyebrows in my congregation!) I was immediately accused by an evangelical Christian in the community of teaching reincarnation. The sad thing is that everyone in the class knew that the Tao Te Ching does not teach reincarnation. Anyone who had ever read the Tao Te Ching would know that. All that accusation did was reveal the ignorance and arrogance of a Christian who was willing to judge a book (one of the greatest spiritual books ever written!) without ever opening it. I was trying to build bridges between the Christian community and people who were "spiritual but not religious," who did not come to church. But that evangelical Christian only succeeded in confirming the stereotype of Christians as ignorant, hypocritical and judgmental.

During my college and seminary years I took it upon myself to study the scriptures and teachings of the major religions of the world. I have continued that practice during my years of ministry. I have not only read the Bible many times, I have also read the entire Quran four times. I have read the Tao Te Ching countless times and even published a Christian version of it. [69] I have read the Bhagavad Gita, the Vedas, and the Upanishads. I have read many of the Buddhist sutras. I have even read the entire Book of Mormon, much to the amazement of the young missionaries who come to my door. I have made it an aim to be well-informed about the religious teachings of other faiths. It seems only fair if I want them to listen the claims of my faith.

I encourage you to do the same. Why should atheists and agnostics be the most informed people about religious matters? Why shouldn't Christians hold that honor? What I have learned in my study of the world's religious traditions is that Christians do not have a monopoly on truth, morality or spirituality. They certainly do not have a monopoly on sincere religious devotion and self-sacrifice.

In my reading I have discovered the fingerprints of God on many of the scriptures of the world's religions. It has made me more humble about my own religion, as well as more confident that God has never left himself without a witness among the peoples of the earth, as the apostle Paul is reported to have said. (Acts 14:16-17)

The best gift that you can give your pastor is to educate yourself about the Bible, as well as the bibles of other peoples and faiths. Learn about how our Bible came to be, and why so many books were left out of our Bible. Do a study of alternative forms of Christianity in the early centuries of our religion. It will give you a whole new perspective on today's Christianity. Only when we have educated ourselves about our own faith (and other's faiths) can we speak intelligently to those looking for faith.

OPEN YOUR HEART

Open your heart to your pastor. Sympathize with him. (Sympathize means "to feel or suffer with.") Empathize with him. (Empathize means to "to feel in," in the sense of imagining oneself in another's position.) The ministry is a lonely profession. There is often no one in a church that a pastor can commiserate with. Be that person, as much as possible. But be sure to keep everything he says to you confidential. If you can't do that, then don't do it at all. Nothing discourages a pastor more than betrayal of trust.

See it as your ministry to minister to your pastor. Every pastor needs a pastor. Be that person. Do not criticize, no matter what. That does not mean that you think everything he says and does is perfect. It just means that you will let someone else be his critic.

There will be more than enough people willing to do that job. You can take the road less traveled. Decide that it is your job to support your pastor in all circumstances. Encourage him. Praise him. Advocate for him when it comes to financial compensation, vacation time, continuing education, and sabbaticals. Don't leave that up to a Pastoral Relations Committee.

Your pastor needs a few people that will be on his side, even when he does not deserve it. See it as your ministry to express unconditional love for him. Consider it your spiritual discipline or spiritual practice. Perhaps recruit another person or two to join you in that ministry. Pray for him daily. Send emails or notes of praise during the year. Praise him in front of others, especially those who think badly of him.

If you genuinely open your heart to your pastor, you will have his undying gratitude, and you will have won a friend for life. In the process you will get a glimpse into the world of professional Christian ministry. Blessed are those who love their pastor even when he is unlovable.

Open your heart to other people. Pick a group of people that you will embrace with the love of Christ. It could be visitors to the church. They are too often ignored, even though they are the only ones who can cause the church to grow.

When I retired two years ago, my wife and I began a search for a new church. Even though we remained in the community and loved the church that I served as pastor, it did not feel right to me to remain part of the congregation while they were looking for a new pastor. It was too easy for people to look to me for pastoral guidance and support. So we went looking for a new church. For a year we attended nearly every Protestant church within a 40 minute drive of our rural home.

It was an eye-opening experience. You would be surprised how often we were ignored by everyone in the congregations that we visited. Often no one spoke to us, welcomed us, or shook our hand. We filled out visitor cards or signed the guest book in every church we visited (the ones that had visitor's cards and books.) Only once did a pastor call us and offer to visit our home. Guess which church we attend now!

It amazed me how inhospitable most churches are to newcomers to the worship service. You could be the person to change that. Don't leave it up to the pastor or a committee. I can tell you from experience that they won't do it.

See it as your ministry to look for new faces every Sunday. Introduce yourself. Inquire if it is the first time they are there. Introduce them to others in the congregation – especially of the same age. Bring them up to the pastor and introduce them. If they return to church, then repeat it all again until they are integrated into the church or they decide that your church is not for them.

In other words be friendly. Unfortunately most churches aren't. You can be the face of Christian love. The song is true that people know we are Christians by our love. It is one of the few things Jesus commands us to do – to love our neighbor and to love our Christian sisters and brothers. If you do that your pastor will be forever grateful.

OPEN YOUR DOORS

Open your church doors to the community. Years ago I interviewed with an urban church in Cincinnati, Ohio, which was searching for a new pastor. I looked through the demographic information that they provided about the church and community. It was a declining white church in an increasingly black neighborhood. Nearly all the church members lived in the suburbs and commuted several miles to church each Sunday.

In my discussions with the search committee I pointed out that the only way their church could grow (and the only way I would serve as their pastor) was if they intentionally reached out to the African American population surrounding the church. Even then, I confided in them, it would not be easy for a white church to integrate successfully without being willing to adopt elements of African American worship. The chairman responded grim-faced, "Our doors are open. If they want to come, they can come." Needless to say I did not accept their offer to be their pastor.

There is only one way for your pastor to succeed in her ministry at your church. And that is if your church is willing to open its doors to the community. I served an urban church in Lowell, Massachusetts, for a few years. It opened its doors to the community. It opened its church to immigrant groups, to people of different cultural backgrounds and languages. It opened its doors to twelve step groups of every kind.

Like the Cincinnati church, the church was a white congregation in a changing neighborhood. But they intentionally reached out to the community. They invited a Cambodian congregation to share their building. The two congregations worshipped together monthly for communion, shared a Sunday School, and had fellowship meals together. The church opened its doors to the community and it thrived. The last time I visited the church, there were four different ethnic congregations in the building worshipping in four different languages! The church has succeeded in fulfilling the promise of the Great Commission.

Your church might not be in an ethnically diverse setting, but your community is diverse in other ways. All it takes is a willingness to think outside the box. With open minds and open hearts and open doors, a church can thrive. But it takes some people who are willing to make it happen.

OPEN YOUR EYES AND EARS

No book is written in a vacuum, and this book is no exception. This book was written in the summer of 2018, while the country was shaken by repeated revelations of sexual abuse of children and assault of women in many segments of society. 2018 is the year of the #MeToo movement, followed by #ChurchToo and #NunsToo. It was publically revealed that sexual assault is rampant in American society and in the church.

As I mentioned in the previous chapter, while writing this book a grand jury in Pennsylvania published its report detailing seven decades of sexual assault and abuse of over a thousand children by over three hundred priests. But it was actually worse than that. The report says, "We believe that the real number of children whose records were lost or who were afraid ever to come forward is in the thousands."

The report goes on to say, "Priests were raping little boys and girls, and the men of God who were responsible for them not only did nothing; they hid it all. For decades. Monsignors, auxiliary bishops, bishops, archbishops, cardinals have mostly been protected; many, including some named in this report, have been promoted." The details of the rapes and abuse mentioned in the report are too graphic and disturbing for me to repeat.

That report covers six Catholic dioceses in Pennsylvania, including the Pittsburgh diocese, where I lived for thirteen years and pastored a Baptist church. I guess that is why the report affected me so deeply. While serving in the Pittsburgh area in the early 2000's I had a confrontation with a local Catholic priest, who was part of the ecumenical clergy group in our town. We disagreed on a number of theological and ethical issues, but the issue that I was most vocal about was the developing story of "pedophile priests." I argued – too strenuously for my ministerial colleagues – that the Roman Catholic Church was not being transparent and was not reporting and prosecuting cases as they should.

My views became public when I wrote an article in June 2002 on the subject for my church newsletter, which I sent to all of the clergy members in our town. It caused a crisis in the Christian community of our small western Pennsylvania town sixteen years ago, when ecumenical relations between Protestants and Catholics were already shaky. (See Appendix 1 for a copy of the article.)

My Protestant colleagues called a special meeting of the Ministerium (as we called our ecumenical clergy group) at a local Methodist church where they expected me to apologize for my criticism of the Catholic Church. I refused to recant. So a few of the Protestant minsters publicly apologized on my behalf, assuring the three priests in attendance that I did not speak for them or for the majority of ministers in town. Coincidentally (or perhaps not) the local parish priest, who had confronted me on this issue, was reassigned to another parish a couple of months later.

I have no idea if that parish was involved in the abuse of children. In looking through the list of Pittsburgh diocese priests named in the grand jury report, none looked familiar. Furthermore I confess that I was arrogant about my theological views at the time, and I was self-righteous in my attitude toward the Catholic Church. But I do not apologize for my condemnation of the Catholic Church's handling of child abuse, and it turns out that my suspicions about the Pittsburgh diocese were more accurate than I imagined.

The abuse of children is not limited to the Catholic Church. While writing this book, Paige Patterson was fired as president of the Southwestern Baptist Theological Seminary for lying to the seminary board about a 2003 rape allegation that came before him at Southeastern Baptist Theological Seminary, which Patterson had previously led, as well as emails surrounding a 2015 rape allegation at Southwestern. This is just one example of a series of revelations about sexual misconduct involving Southern Baptist churches and seminaries. As a result in July 2018, the Southern Baptist Convention announced the creation of a study group to develop strategies for combatting sexual abusers and ministering to their victims.

Megachurch pastor Bill Hybels, a high profile evangelical, was forced from his position at Willow Creek Community Church over allegations of sexual misconduct. A couple of months later the church's board of elders and both lead pastors, who had succeeded Hybels, all resigned over the mismanagement of the investigation of the allegations against Hybels dating from the 1980's.

From all accounts it appears that this wave of resignations and accusations is not over. Sexual abuse and assault in Protestant and evangelical churches has probably been just as pervasive, though less publicized, as in the Catholic Church. Boz Tchividjian, a grandson of evangelist Billy Graham who heads GRACE, a ministry working to combat sexual abuse in churches, said, "I really believe churches need to enter into a season of lament, acknowledging decades of failure to understand, address and confront these horrors."[70]

I have had to deal with the sexual assault of children in one of the churches that I served. By the grace of God I handled the accusation swiftly and thoroughly. A young man privately shared with me an incident involving the chairman of our church's board of trustees. I immediately confronted the trustee in person in the presence of the local police chief. Afterwards the police chief and I immediately went to the church moderator to officially inform the church leadership. The trustee had been a Boy Scout leader who had been sexually assaulting boys for decades. He confessed to his crimes and was convicted and sentenced. He had not been working with children in our church, and therefore evaded the vetting process, but that did not stop him from abusing children in the church.

I thanked the young man who suspected something was wrong and had the courage to tell me. He saw something and said something, and I am very grateful. You do a great service for your pastor when you keep your eyes and ears open to anything that does not appear right involving the treatment of children (and women) in the congregation.

As they say about terrorism, "If you see something, say something." Child abuse is a form of terrorism. It is literally terrifying for the victims. Churches are a refuge for the vulnerable. For that reason it can be a hunting ground for sexual predators. Open your eyes and ears to the possibility of sexual assault and abuse. Don't be under the illusion that it can't happen in your church. When you see something suspicious, open your mouth and say something!

As disturbing as abuse is, the cover-up of abuse is just as bad. Make sure there is no cover-up in your church. Don't let anything be pushed under the rug, no matter how devastating it may be to the reputation of your church. The reputation of your church will be far worse if you do not report it promptly.

If you suspect your pastor of inappropriate behavior or covering up inappropriate behavior, call the police. I wish I could tell you to contact the church authorities, but I no longer trust those in authority in the church to handle this correctly. Church hierarchies have proven that they are unreliable in reporting abuse to the authorities. Just go straight to the police. That is what I did. And if assault or abuse has happened to you, tell someone you trust, and report it to the authorities now.

CONCLUSION

There are a lot of things that your pastor will not tell you. Some of these have to do with Christian ministry. When it comes to ministry, your pastor needs your understanding and support.

Your pastor has also not told everything you should know about the Bible. The Bible is not what most people think it is. I had one couple in a premarital counseling session ask me where they could find the Christian wedding ceremony in the Bible. They obviously had never opened a Bible.

My experience is that most people assume the Bible is a volume of ethical lessons and morality tales, like Aesop's fables for Christians. It is far from that. In fact there are more immorality tales than morality tales in the Bible. Many of the examples of faith in the Bible are morally troubling, such as Abraham's willingness to sacrifice his young son Isaac by slitting his throat.

Your pastor likely won't tell you about the ongoing battle between Christianity and science. Frankly it is embarrassing. He might hesitate to overtly inform the congregation that evolution is a fact, so as not to alienate the creationist members of the church. But silence on such issues just keeps the church in the dark ages.

It is likely your pastor has not told you about the history of Christian theology. Christian doctrines that are accepted as "gospel truth" today – beliefs such as the Trinity, the Virgin Birth, and the bodily resurrection of Jesus - were just one set of possibilities in the early centuries of Christianity. If early church history had unfolded slightly differently, Christians today might worship two gods or thirty gods.

Instead of salvation by grace through faith in Jesus, we might proclaim the necessity of keeping the Law as found in the Old Testament. Instead of believing in Jesus as the only begotten Son of God, we might accept him as just a man. Or we might believe that he was a purely spiritual being without a physical body. The development of Christian theology was a complex evolutionary process that involved the extinction of many alternative forms of Christianity.

Your pastor probably has not told you that the Bible condones slavery, that Jesus taught pacifism, or that sexism pervades the Scriptures. There are lots of things your pastor has not told you. I have told you a few of them in this book. You pastor can tell you a lot more, if you let her. Get to know your pastor, and she might share with you some interesting truths. Christianity is much stranger than you think.

APPENDIX 1

The Baptist Beacon, the Monthly Newsletter of the First Baptist Church, Rochester, Pennsylvania, June 2002.

Zero Tolerance

All eyes are on Rome. The sexual abuse of thousands of children in America by hundreds of Roman Catholic priests over decades is headline news day after day, and rightly so. It is scandalous! I suspect that these who have been caught are only the tip of the iceberg. How many more are hiding, scared that their past will be revealed?

Personally I have not been this upset by a religious news story for many years. I pray it will not go away until it is dealt with openly, publicly and thoroughly. I pray that this will be a "wake-up call" for all Roman Catholics. No longer can the Roman hierarchy hide the serial sexual abuse of children. No longer can they ignore the complaints of parents. No longer can they move predatory priests from parish to parish. This is the day of reckoning for Rome.

True Christians, born again of the Spirit of God, do not commit the type of heinous crimes these priests are guilty of. "Whoever abides in Him does not sin. Whoever sins has neither seen Him nor known Him. Little children, let no one deceive you. He who practices righteousness is righteous, just as He is righteous. He who sins is of the devil, for the devil has sinned from the beginning. For this purpose the Son of God was manifested, that He might destroy the works of the devil. 9Whoever has been born of God does not sin, for His seed remains in him; and he cannot sin, because he has been born of God." (I John 3:6-9)

True Christians do not cover up for these criminals and do not conveniently "forget" when put under oath in a court of law. "And this is the condemnation, that the light has come into the world, and men loved darkness rather than light, because their deeds were evil. For everyone practicing evil hates the light and does not come to the light, lest his deeds should be exposed. But he who does the truth comes to the light, that his deeds may be clearly seen, that they have been done in God." (John 3:19-21)

True Christians do not put the "church" above innocent victims. "For as you have done it to the least of these my brethren you have done to me." Nor do they reject restitution made to victims because it is too financially costly. Better to lose all, than to lose your soul. "For what will it profit a man if he gains the whole world, and loses his own soul." (Mark 8:36)

Jesus said that what has been done in secret will be shouted from the rooftops. "Be on your guard against the yeast of the Pharisees, which is hypocrisy. There is nothing concealed that will not be disclosed, or hidden that will not be made known. What you have said in the dark will be heard in the daylight, and what you have whispered in the ear in the inner rooms will be proclaimed from the roofs." (Luke 12:1-3)

His words are coming true. You will know them by their fruits. It will be revealed to all with eyes to see if these religious leaders are children of light or darkness. And if the leaders walk in darkness, what hope is there for the followers?" And if the blind leads the blind, both will fall into a ditch." (Matthew 15:14)

It is time for crimes to be paid for and people in high places to be exposed, punished and imprisoned. Will Rome be on the side of righteousness, justice and the innocent, or protect the powerful? The answer will reveal the true nature of the Roman church and determine relations between Catholics and evangelicals for years to come.

Your troubled pastor,

Marshall

OTHER BOOKS BY MARSHALL DAVIS

Understanding Revelation

The Evolution of Easter: How the Historical Jesus Became the Risen Christ

The Seeker's Journey: A Contemporary Retelling of Pilgrim's Progress

The Parables of Jesus: American Paraphrase Version

Thank God for Atheists: What Christians Can Learn from the New Atheism

Experiencing God Directly: The Way of Christian Nonduality

The Tao of Christ: A Christian Version of the Tao Te Ching

Living Presence: A Guide to Everyday Awareness of God

More Than a Purpose: An Evangelical Response to Rick Warren and the Megachurch Movement

The Baptist Church Covenant: Its History and Meaning

A People Called Baptist: An Introduction to Baptist History & Heritage

The Practice of the Presence of God in Modern English by Brother Lawrence, translated by Marshall Davis

The Gospel of Solomon: The Christian Message in the Song of Solomon

Esther

The Hidden Ones

ABOUT THE AUTHOR

Marshall Davis is an ordained American Baptist minister who has served churches in New Hampshire, Massachusetts, Pennsylvania, Illinois and Kentucky during his forty year ministry as a pastor.

He holds a Bachelor of Arts degree in Religion from Denison University, as well Master of Divinity and Doctor of Ministry degrees from the Southern Baptist Theological Seminary, Louisville, Kentucky.

Having retired from fulltime pastoral ministry, nowadays he spends most days at his 18th century home in a small New Hampshire village in the White Mountains. He writes nearly every day, preaches occasionally, and plays with grandchildren often.

Find out more at amazon.com/Marshall-Davis/e/B001K8Y0RU/

Or visit revmdavis.blogspot.com/

ENDNOTES

[1] LifeWay Research, "Churchgoers Stick Around for Theology, Not Music or Preachers" June 26, 2018, https://lifewayresearch.com/2018/06/26/churchgoers-stick-around-for-theology-not-music-or-preachers/, accessed July 5, 2018

[2] Jeff Brumley, "Researchers discover another reason Americans leave church," Baptist News Global, July 3, 2018. https://baptistnews.com/article/researchers-discover-another-reason-americans-leave-church, accessed July 9, 2018.

[3] Barna Group; "Gen Z: The Culture, Beliefs and Motivations Shaping the Next Generation" (January 23, 2018)

[4] Charles Templeton, Farewell to God: My Reasons for Rejecting the Christian Faith (Kindle Locations 171-186. McClelland & Stewart. Kindle Edition.

[5] Billy Graham, Just As I Am: The Autobiography of Billy Graham, Harper Collins Worldwide, 1997, page 139

[6] Mark Kelly, "Pastors' work hours tallied in new survey" Baptist Press, January 06, 2010. http://www.bpnews.net/31993

[7] Fred Lehr, Clergy Burnout: Recovering from the 70 hour Work Week and Other Self-Defeating Practices, Augsburg Fortress, 2006, p. 4.

[8] Sarah Eekhoff Zylstra, "1 in 4 Pastors Have Struggled with Mental Illness, Finds LifeWay and Focus on the Family, Christianity Today, September 22, 2014. https://www.christianitytoday.com/news/2014/september/1-in-4-pastors-have-mental-illness-lifeway-focus-on-family.html , accessed July 17, 2018.

[9] Sarah Eekhoff Zylstra, "Why Pastors Are Committing Suicide" The Gospel Coalition, November 23, 2016, https://www.thegospelcoalition.org/article/why-pastors-are-committing-suicide/

[10] J. Cuesta, Why Are So Many Pastors Committing Suicide? https://praisedc.com/author/jcuesta1/; and Amy Frykholm, "The Pastors Are Alright", Christian Century , May 9, 2018, p. 22.

[11] Amy Frykholm, "The Pastors Are Alright", Christian Century , May 9, 2018, p. 22.

[12] Amy Frykholm, "The Pastors Are Alright", Christian Century , May 9, 2018, p. 23.

[13] I am indebted to many of John Sanford's categories in his book Ministry Burnout, Westminster John Knox Press (September 1, 1992)

for the framework of this section.

[14] Harry Bruinius, "Churches struggle with their #MeToo moment," Christian Science Monitor, April 20, 2018. https://www.csmonitor.com/USA/Politics/2018/0420/Churches-struggle-with-their-MeToo-moment

[15] G. Lloyd Rediger, *Clergy Killers: Guidance for Pastors and Churches Under Attack*, Westminster John Knox Press, 1997, p. 2.

[16] Guy Greenfield, *The Wounded Minister: Healing from and Preventing Personal Attacks*, Baker Books, 2001, pp. 14,16.

[17] In addition the Greek word for "other" used here is not the common word allos (ἄλλος), which means "another of the same kind," which we would expect if he was counting Paul's letters among the scriptures. Neither is it the other word for other: heteros (ἕτερος), which means "another of a different kind." It is instead worthed loipos (λοιπός) which is the more general term which could mean either. The author seems to be grouping Paul's writings and sacred Scripture together under a broader category. This is supported by the fact that the word translated "Scripture" grapha (γραφή) just means "writing" – any type of writing. The author might be referring to other writings that were circulating among the churches. There were a lot of letters, gospels, apocalypses, and other Christian writings in circulation in the first century which never made it into the Bible. In fact Paul mentions forgeries written in his name that were circulating (2 Thessalonians 2:2).

[18] McKim, DK, Westminster dictionary of theological terms, Westminster John Knox Press, 1996.

[19] Joseph Campbell and the Power Of Myth, Ep. 2: The Message of the Myth, June 22, 1988. https://billmoyers.com/content/ep-2-joseph-campbell-and-the-power-of-myth-the-message-of-the-myth/

[20] Gallup, "In U.S., 42% Believe Creationist View of Human Origins," Frank Newport, June 2, 2014, https://news.gallup.com/poll/170822/believe-creationist-view-human-origins.aspx

[21] Proverbs 8; Psalm 33; Psalm 104; Jeremiah 10; Jeremiah 4; Isaiah 28; Isaiah 40; Isaiah 45; Isaiah 11; Hosea 2; Genesis 1; Genesis 2; Psalm 89; Psalm 8; Psalm 19; Psalm 102:25; Job 26; Job 28; Job 38; John 1; Revelation 21

[22] Roger Forster and Paul Marston, Reason, Science and Faith, Monarch Books © 1999, p. 198,

23 "Scientific Theory," Wikipedia, https://en.wikipedia.org/wiki/Scientific_theory, accessed July 21, 2018.

24 Lawrence M. Krauss, *A Universe from Nothing: Why There Is Something Rather Than Nothing,* Free Press, January 10, 2012.

25 Skeptical Science, "The 97% consensus on global warming" http://www.skepticalscience.com/global-warming-scientific-consensus.htm Accessed July 23, 2018.

26 "Religion and Views on Climate and Energy Issues" Cary Funk and Becka A. Alper, Pew Research Center, http://www.pewinternet.org/2015/10/22/religion-and-views-on-climate-and-energy-issues/ accessed July 23, 2018.

27 Robert Knop, "The Difference Between Religion and Woo" Aug 21 2010, Published by Galactic Interactions, A Blog about Physics, Astronomy, and Many Other Things. http://galacticinteractions.scientopia.org/2010/08/21/the-difference-between-religion-and-woo/ accessed July 23, 2018.

28 Skeptico, "What is Woo?" http://skeptico.blogs.com/skeptico/woo-woo.html accessed July 23, 2018

29 For my discussion of Ebionites, Marcionites, and Gnostics, I am indebted to Bart Ehrman's books *Lost Christianities: The Battles for Scripture and the Faiths We Never Knew*, Oxford University Press. Kindle Edition.

30 The synoptic gospels are Mark, Matthew, and Luke.

31 A term coined by Albert Schweitzer in his 1906 classic, *The Quest of the Historical Jesus.*

32 Ehrman, Bart D.. Lost Christianities: The Battles for Scripture and the Faiths We Never Knew (p. 100). Oxford University Press. Kindle Edition.

33 See Wikipedia article on "Ebionites" https://en.wikipedia.org/wiki/Ebionites

34 Fellowship Church, Winter Springs, Florida.

35 Both of these quotations from the Pseudo-Clementines, I got from Ehrman, Bart D.. Lost Christianities: The Battles for Scripture and the Faiths We Never Knew (pp. 183-4). Oxford University Press. Kindle Edition.

36 In this section I am indebted to the Wikipedia article "Antisemitism and the New Testament", https://en.wikipedia.org/wiki/Antisemitism_and_the_New_Testament , accessed July 27, 2018.

[37] R. Alan Culpepper, "Anti-Judaism in the Fourth Gospel as a Theological Problem for Christian Interpreters," in Reimund Bieringer, Didier Pollefeyt, Frederique Vandecasteele-Vanneuville (eds.), Anti-Judaism and the Fourth Gospel, Publisher Westminster John Knox Press, 2001 pp.61-82, p.64.

[38] Ehrman, Bart D., Lost Christianities: The Battles for Scripture and the Faiths We Never Knew (pp. 108-109). Oxford University Press. Kindle Edition.

[39] Clement of Alexandria's Excerpts from Theodotus, 78.2., quoted in Ehrman, Bart D.. Lost Christianities: The Battles for Scripture and the Faiths We Never Knew (p. 269). Oxford University Press. Kindle Edition.

[40] What Do Americans Believe About Jesus? 5 Popular Beliefs, Barna Update, Articles in Faith & Christianity • April 1, 2015, https://www.barna.com/research/what-do-americans-believe-about-jesus-5-popular-beliefs/ accessed August 1, 2018.

[41] Hebrews 4:15; 1 Peter 2:22; 2 Corinthians 5:21; 1 John 3:5.

[42] Shane Morris, Survey Finds Most American Christians Are Actually Heretics, The Federalist, October 10, 2016, http://thefederalist.com/2016/10/10/survey-finds-american-christians-actually-heretics/ accessed August 1, 2018.

[43] Yuriy Stasyuk, "Crazy Theology: What The Early Church Fathers Believed" The Reluctant Skeptic, http://yuriystasyuk.com/crazy-theology-what-the-early-church-fathers-believed/ which includes quotes from the church fathers backing the statements.

[44] Apostles Creed - Book of Common Prayer, 1662.

[45] This is also known as the "Nicene-Constantinopolitan Creed," because of a belief that it was adopted at the Second Ecumenical Council held in Constantinople in 381 as a modification of the original Nicene Creed of 325. It came to be commonly known simply as the "Nicene Creed."

[46] Ehrman, Bart D.. How Jesus Became God: The Exaltation of a Jewish Preacher from Galilee (Kindle Location 675). HarperCollins. Kindle Edition.

[47] Kaufmann Kohler, Emil G. Hirsch, "Son of God" Jewish Encyclopedia, 1906, http://www.jewishencyclopedia.com/articles/13912-son-of-god accessed August 3, 2018.

[48] C.S. Lewis, Mere Christianity (1952; Harper Collins: 2001) 163.

[49] Barna Group Inc., "State of the Church 2016,"

https://www.barna.com/research/state-church-2016/ accessed August 6, 2018.

[50] http://www.pewforum.org/2017/08/31/after-500-years-reformation-era-divisions-have-lost-much-of-their-potency/ accessed August 6, 2018.

[51] This section is adapted from the Introduction of my book *Understanding Revelation,* 2017. Kindle Edition.

[52] This section is an adaptation of two sections "Hell is Biblical" and "Taking the Sting out of Hell" from Chapter 5, "Questioning the New Testament God" of my book, *Thank God for Atheists: What Christians Can Learn from the New Atheism,* 2017, (Kindle edition).

[53] Quoted in "Ignoring Yahweh's Judgment In Politically Correct America!" by Lee Webb, https://www.worthychristianforums.com/topic/11190-the-disappearance-of-hell/

[54] http://www.reasonablefaith.org/can-a-loving-god-send-people-to-hell-the-craig-bradley-debate, accessed August 11, 2016.

[55] Kate Shellnutt, March 28, 2018, "No Lie: Americans Still Ascribe to the Ten Commandments" Christianity Today, https://www.christianitytoday.com/news/2018/march/ten-commandments-survey-lying-murder-deseret-news-yougov.html. See also Albert Mohler, 'The Scandal of Biblical Illiteracy: It's Our Problem" January 20, 2016, https://albertmohler.com/2016/01/20/the-scandal-of-biblical-illiteracy-its-our-problem-4/

[56] Most And Least Religious Cities In America, Huffington Post, 05/18/2012, Updated Dec 06, 2017, https://www.huffingtonpost.com/2012/05/18/most-and-least-religious-cities_n_1522644.html#slide=989786

[57] David Briggs "No Time For Crime: Study Finds More Religious Communities Have Lower Rates Of Black, White and Latino Violence" https://www.huffingtonpost.com/david-briggs/no-time-for-crime-study-f_b_4384046.html

[58] Christianity and the Civil War, Christianity Today, https://www.christianitytoday.com/history/issues/issue-33/christianity-and-civil-war-did-you-know.html Accessed August 12, 2018.

[59] Bradley Burston, "This Is Zionism as Racism. This Is Israel at 70" Haaretz, Apr 04, 2018, https://www.haaretz.com/opinion/.premium-this-is-zionism-as-racism-this-is-israel-at-70-1.5975641

[60] Allan Brownfeld, "Israel at 70: An Alarming Growth of Racism And

Intolerance" Washington Report on Middle East Affairs, June/July 2018, pp. 40-41, https://www.wrmea.org/2018-june-july/israel-at-70-an-alarming-growth-of-racism-and-intolerance.html

[61] "Knesset Speaker: Bible is Jews' Deed to This Land" Israel Today, February 05, 2015, http://www.israeltoday.co.il/NewsItem/tabid/178/nid/25983/Default.aspx

[62] Emily Scott, "The Bible's #MeToo Problem" (June 16, 2018) https://www.nytimes.com/2018/06/16/opinion/sunday/women-the-bible-metoo.html

[63] https://lifewayresearch.com/2017/04/25/lifeway-research-americans-are-fond-of-the-bible-dont-actually-read-it/

[64] Albert Mohler, 'The Scandal of Biblical Illiteracy: It's Our Problem" January 20, 2016, https://albertmohler.com/2016/01/20/the-scandal-of-biblical-illiteracy-its-our-problem-4/

[65] "State of the Bible 2018: Seven Top Findings," Research Releases in Faith & Christianity, July 10, 2018, https://www.barna.com/research/state-of-the-bible-2018-seven-top-findings/

[66] "Why We Left the Church" https://yuriystasyuk.com/5-big-myths-about-why-people-leave-their-religion/

[67] Pew Research Center, U.S. Religious Knowledge Survey Executive Summary, September 28, 2010, http://www.pewforum.org/2010/09/28/u-s-religious-knowledge-survey/

[68] Ibid.

[69] Out of that experience came my book *The Tao of Christ: A Christian Version of the Tao Te Ching*.

[70] David Crary, "Evangelicals confront sex abuse problems in #MeToo era," The Associated Press 08/18/18, http://www.morningjournal.com/article/MJ/20180818/NEWS/180819470

Made in the USA
Coppell, TX
16 July 2021